How to Get Your Joy Back!

A WOMEN'S GUIDE TO MIDLIFE CAREER TRANSFORMATION

Maria Luchsinger

The Women's Career Transformation Network

The Women's Career Transformation Network - P. O. Box 12236 - Everett, WA 98206 www.marialuchsinger.com

Ordering Information: Quantity sales. Special discounts are available on quantity purchases by corporations, associations, and others.

Publisher's Cataloging-In-Publication Data (Prepared by The Donohue Group, Inc.)

Names: Luchsinger, Maria.

Title: How to get your joy back! : a women's guide to midlife career transformation / Maria Luchsinger.

Description: First edition. | Everett, WA : The Women's Career Transformation Network, [2017] | Includes bibliographical references and index.

Identifiers: LCCN 2016921484 | ISBN 978-0-9897630-5-9 (paperback) | ISBN 978-0-9991680-1-1 (hardback) | ISBN 978-0-9897630-9-7 (Kindle) | ISBN 978-0-9991680-0-4 (EPub)

Subjects: LCSH: Women--Vocational guidance. | Career changes. | Quality of work life. | Self-realization in women. | Goal (Psychology) | Self-employed women. Classification: LCC HF5382.6 .L83 2017 (print) | LCC HF5382.6 (ebook) | DDC 331.702/082--dc23

Printed in the United States of America

This book is dedicated to the special women in my life who encouraged and inspired me to believe that there is nothing I cannot achieve.

Contents

Just don't give up trying to do what you really want to do.
Where there is love and inspiration, I don't think you can go wrong.

— ELLA FITZGERALD

Introduction

Why I Wrote This Book

I wrote this book because I believe there are too many women who are feeling hopeless about their current life and career situations. I would like to be an encouragement to others who have been through my similar life experiences. You may be going through a divorce with children, trying to find the best way to get back into the workforce. You may be deciding that you have had enough of a toxic work environment. Or you may be thinking that now is the time to do work that helps other people and is important and meaningful to you.

In addition to being a teacher and certified life coach, I am also a wife, a mother, and a grandmother. I have been through marriage and divorce. I have been alone and on call 24/7 raising two children while working full-time for several years through tough economic times. I have known the frustration of trying to find time for myself.

During the course of my over 30 years of work experience, I have had two careers. One in business, working in the financial world of escrow, and one in education. My experience in the education field included managing a licensed child care business of my own that included my children when they were young and working as an elementary school teacher in the public school system.

At the end of 2010, I was working in a stressful job in the commercial escrow department of a title insurance company that was going through a merger. Up until the last part of my almost seven years with the company, I had been able to leave a half hour early to catch a train or bus home because I had a long commute. When the new management took over, I was told that I must stay until 5:00 p.m. This meant that I would not arrive home until 6:45 p.m. every night.

I was getting exhausted, and I thought there must be a better way. I transformed my own life by looking at the places where I experienced joy and what my strengths were and taking actions toward accomplishing my dreams.

I took inventory of what I had to offer the world and found that I wanted to use my creativity, energy, and talent to help people. This led to the publishing of the Sammy the Centipede series of children's books on health and wellness and renewing my teaching credentials to become a substitute teacher. Also taking into account my over 30 years of work experience, I thought about how I had been encouraging women all my life. This led to certification as a life coach with the desire to help empower women to transform their careers and have lives filled with joy instead of frustration.

I am here to show you that having a vision of where you want to go is the ultimate secret of life. My purpose is to help reconnect you to your joy and lead you to a transformed life full of freedom and purpose.

Whatever you envision – your entire being, consciously and unconsciously, will strive to achieve.

There are so many resources available to us today; it is an exciting time to be alive. This book is about possibilities. It will help you make a mind shift from your everyday thinking patterns. It could lead you to a personal revolution.

It is my goal to help you reach the dreams and goals that you have been thinking about deep down in your soul. The ones that maybe nobody supports, but that you are confident you can achieve.

How to Use This Book

Part I

The first section is divided up into chapters that describe where you may be in your start to this journey of re-invention. Start by picking the one that resonates with where you are now on your quest for zest. All of the chapters in the first section lead to the beginning of Section II. You may want to go back and read the other chapters at a later time, but for now, start with the one that fits your situation the best right now.

Part II

At the end of the section that you pick as a point to begin, you will be directed to the Wheel of Life Worksheet in Chapter 6, Part II. This section contains the process you will use to reconnect with your joy, confirm your strengths and choose a new direction when you get to the Personal Goals Worksheet.

Part III

Contains information about various paths that you may decide to take after you have considered where you want to go on your new journey.

Resources

This guide contains information including inspiring people along with their books and/or web sites for reference that will help you on the path you choose.

This book is designed to support you on your journey to craft a career that will emphasize your sense of purpose and boost your knowledge of how to achieve the freedom that you crave.

PART ONE

Where Are You Now?

CHAPTER 1

Same Career for Many Years

Why in the World am I Still Here?

Joan had been working in administrative support for a few years, with an endless list of tasks to perform from a group of realtors. She began to think how she could use her skills to do work that was meaningful to her personally. She decided to use her abilities to benefit a nonprofit organization that lined up with her values. This led to her greater happiness knowing that her work was benefiting a cause that she cared about.

Besides an office job, you may feel stuck in manufacturing, hospitality, healthcare, or one of a myriad of other fields that don't feel like a good fit for you now. You may be wondering why you have stayed so long in your current position and there doesn't seem to be anywhere to go from here. Your thoughts might revolve around the fact that you do your job well, but there is no path to advancement; you feel trapped because you need to make money for your family or don't think you have the necessary skills to get a better job. Wherever you are working, you feel that it is time for a change.

You may love your company and just want to change direction. In order to advance in the job you have now, you might consider taking a leadership role in a current project or one where you get to use skills that aren't necessarily linked to your current job. Find a way to save your company money and implement the changes or propose the changes to the right person in charge. People who implement money saving strategies usually get noticed.

Use networking skills as referenced in Chapter 14 to see what upcoming jobs within your company may be coming available and tailor your education to that. If you feel you lack skills, there are many ways to get them. Your company might have training that you could take advantage of, or you could check with online programs from universities. Your local community college will probably have night classes that can help you. If you feel you can innovate a new position that fits you better, figure out how it will benefit the company and go see your manager.

What have you got to lose? If they don't go for it, they will see that you have taken the initiative. Depending on how well your ideas were received, you can decide if this is the place for you, or if you want to consider moving on.

Is it time to try something new? Maybe you are bored to death. Maybe you are just not the right fit for your job anymore, or you have a toxic work environment. When the children are gone from home, it causes many of us to wonder if now is the time to venture out into new horizons. Is there something that you have wanted to do for a long time? Do you have the life experience now to venture out into your own business? Maybe you are thinking of a partnership with another like-minded person.

Having a long time career is the perfect springboard to try something different because you can gradually shift your focus to the new beginning while having the financial stability to do so. If you are determined to leave your job, you will need to research where you might want to go well ahead of time. Be sure you have money saved in the bank or a way to pay your bills before you leave. When you do leave, give at least two weeks' notice as you may need a recommendation from your boss or need to return to the company later on.

The job market has changed greatly, and we are now living in a global economy. The possibilities are endless. You are your own brand. That brand could take on many different forms. You may be able to start a business doing something that you have loved for years. You may find a company that has the job that you have always wanted, and you know you have the qualifications. All you need to do is figure out what it is you really want to do, make a plan, and take action!

Before you make that plan, take a look at the Wheel of Life in Chapter 6, Part II to see where you are in your life now and make plans to get you where you want to be.

CHAPTER 2

Returning to Work After a Long Break

How Do I Get Back In?

Getting back into the workforce in our present economy may require online savvy for job searches, networking, and social media, along with current technological or technical skills to compete for your desired job.

You may also find employers who will give you a job, but you will need to find your own health insurance, life insurance, and plan a way for you to save for retirement. You may have one or two part-time jobs. Because of the shifting economy, when you do find a full-time job, you may not be able to work there for many years as was so usual in the past.

As an older worker, you may have an advantage over a younger one, because older workers tend to be dedicated, punctual, detail-oriented, good listeners, and bring a maturity to the job because of their years of experience. One of the biggest concerns that employers have about hiring older workers is their lack of computer and technology skills. The ability to learn technical skills is a great benefit to have when you are considering returning to the workforce.

Technology is ever changing so check job descriptions carefully for the names of the programs where you need to be proficient. Whether you are working in an office or out in the field recording biological test data, there is always a need for computer skills.

If you don't have training in computer programs like Word, Excel, PowerPoint, Outlook, or Access contained in the Microsoft Office Suite, you will be able to find help online at Alison.com's Microsoft Office training. This is a free course with certification. If you need help with newer versions, go to Lynda.com where you can sign up for a 10-day free trial to use any of the teaching programs they have available. After that, there is economical pricing to continue month to month. You can also check with your local library or community college for books and courses for various training you might need. While you are looking for a job is a great time to take the technology classes that you will need to succeed in the job that you want.

You are probably using technology right now to connect with other people on social media. LinkedIn is one of the best places online to connect with prospective hiring managers. This site is like Facebook for business professionals.

When you fill out your LinkedIn profile, make sure you have a professional headshot. The conversation here is what you would expect in an office environment. Don't hesitate to include professional organizations and associations that you belong to, because you may be able to make connections there too. You can actually follow them on the site, along with major corporations or businesses that you are interested in. You have the possibility of writing articles under your name that will be read by people who visit your site. LinkedIn will give you access to people who would never know you were looking for a job.

Besides, LinkedIn, there are many online job searching sites. One of my favorite web sites for career searching is called TheMuse.com. This web site is a great place to find out about various company cultures, topics of interest to career seekers, and there are job listings for major cities there as well. Most employers have job applicants apply online, and it is frustrating sometimes because you may not hear back from them right away or at all. Some of the top job hunting sites are Indeed, Simply Hired, Monster, and Glassdoor.

If you are looking for a specific field of work, look for job sites that cater to that field. Use Google to enter the name of an unfamiliar site + reviews to see whether the site you found is worth your time. Be sure to look for scams for any listing you find that tells you about a job where you can work from home. Remember to limit your online searching and work on meeting people and building relationships that can lead to job prospects.

It is critical to build relationships through networking. Networking is so important because the saying "It's who you know" has never been more relevant. But how do you network effectively? Networking is not about how many business cards you can collect, but how many relationships you can build and nurture.

Always be real with people and show appreciation for their efforts and any opportunities extended to you. Focus on how you can help them, and by doing so, you will create relationships that will last.

One of the best ways to develop relationships in your immediate area is to join Meetup groups in your city. In order to find one, just Google Meetup + your city or go to Meetup.com. They are a wonderful source of connecting with people who are like-minded. This will give you a natural way to make connections. For instance, if you are an entrepreneur, you can join a group of entrepreneurs, make friends, and gain referrals at the same time. You may be able to collaborate on projects with others in the group.

Many single entrepreneurs love groups like this because it helps them not to feel isolated in their business. You can also join Meetups where your potential clients would attend and start building relationships with Meetup leaders. If you have a hobby, like to hike, or have any other interest, there is probably a Meetup that fits the description. It is possible to belong to several different Meetups which will give you a wide variety of ways to connect with people.

If you don't, why not start a group that centers on your interests? Starting your own Meetup group will give you exposure as a leader in your community. The framework is already set up for you to connect by email and put your events on the calendar. Do not be discouraged if only one or two people show up at first. I started my own group for women's career transformation in my community. When you first go to Meetup.com you can explore all the possibilities there are for different kinds of Meetups on just about any subject. When you are sure what kind of Meetup you want to start, you can click on "Create a Meetup" and then follow the instructions. There might only be a few people sign up at first, and they will probably not all show-up. Plan for a consistent meeting place and time, and you will eventually see your group grow.

There are other effective ways to connect with people. Seek out professional organizations that are of interest to you and join them with the intention of building quality relationships around common interests. Check in with your family and friends who may have connections to people who can help you that you don't even realize.

Reconnect with prior business colleagues to find out the latest news in your industry and see what they know about available jobs. Contact the job center at the college from which you graduated to see what job listings might interest you. They usually know about job opportunities nationwide.

Become a master at connecting people to each other. Think of who you know and then make mutually beneficial introductions. This produces a win for you and for them. These kinds of meetings can produce a kind of synergy that could turn into something positive that you would never expect.

Develop the brand of YOU across social media channels. Associate yourself with organizations and people who are in your target market for a job or who would be good prospects for your products or service in the future.

When you are generous with time and information, you will become known and trusted and develop quality relationships. Relationships that last for years might start at a conference or networking event. When you attend a conference or networking event, be open to striking up conversations with people you don't know. You may get to know something about them from the company listed on their name tag or conversations at the table where you are sitting.

If you find that there may be a common interest, smile and introduce yourself. If you have time while waiting for festivities to begin or at a mixer, ask them about their latest project and talk about what you have been working on lately. You can usually determine whether this will be your only conversation or if you would like to follow up with each other. Take a look at the list of speakers ahead of time, so you can make the best choices and use of your time. You might have a speaker that you have a personal interest in to make a connection. See if they are allowing time at the end of their session for questions and get their contact information. Maybe they wrote a book, and you can pick that up.

Here is a story about how my connections in 2013 led to more connections in 2016. I attended the NAPW (National Association of Professional Women) national conference in New York City in 2013. I met the following amazing women:

Arianna Huffington was a keynote speaker, and she invited us to email her if we had an idea we wanted to discuss. I took her up on this offer and landed an article in the Huffington Post about my decision to find a better way to work after long hours had me totally exhausted.

Dr. Liubov Sichel, a probiotic research specialist. She and I had a lengthy discussion about the health of American families. She became a reviewer for my children's book on nutrition, *Sammy the Centipede Goes to the Market.*

Bridget Diarrassouba and co-founder, Marsha Clarke, who are the founders of New Life Coach, Inc., where I later obtained my life coaching certification.

M. Shannon Hernandez, who told me that my Sammy the Centipede character in my books needed a blog. We kept in touch and in 2016 received the opportunity to be a guest on Shannon's Courageous Living Show which is broadcasted on BLAB.

Because of her introduction to Susan Vernicek, the owner and editor of Identity Magazine, I was invited to speak in a breakout session at the Identity Magazine's Women's Retreat in 2016.

As you can see, as a result of this one conference, I found a reviewer for my nutrition book for children, landed an article in the Huffington

Post, met the coaches who would eventually give me life coach certification, and gained two valuable speaking opportunities. All of these experiences are part of my journey to getting back into the workforce in a way that makes me happy today.

When you attend a conference or networking event, near your home or far away, you never know where one conversation will take you. Be open to helping and listening to people, and it will surprise you where you will end up.

There are additional resources for networking in Chapter 14, but first, go to Chapter 6, do the Wheel of Life Worksheet, and then fill out the Personal Goals Worksheet. This will give you a snapshot of where you are now and a place to make goals that will coincide with returning to the workforce.

RESOURCES

Alison's Microsoft Training. www.alisoncom.

Glassdoor. www.glassdoor.com

Huffington Post. www.huffingtonpost.com

Identity Magazine. www.identitymagazine.net

Indeed. www.indeed.com

LinkedIn. www.linkedin.com

Lynda. www.lynda.com

Meetup. www.Meetup.com

Monster. www.monster.com

National Association of Professional Women. www.napw.com

New Life Coach, Inc. www.newlifecoachinc.org

Simply Hired. www.simplyhired.com

CHAPTER 3

Balancing Career and Family Life

There Is Never Enough Time!

The question is always asked whether a woman can have it all. I agree with the women that say they can - if they maintain balance. What is balance? That means different things to different people. I believe when a person is at peace with their decisions and they are not in a constant state of stress, then they have balance.

Women look for peace in their families when they work. Not all women are in the same situation with regard to raising children. You might be balancing work with children still at home, may be in the process of getting ready to send children out into the world, or you may not have children. This chapter will focus mainly on how to balance life with children still at home.

You might work part-time, have a full-time job because that is where you feel you should be, or not be able to stay home with your children if you wanted to. I have belonged to all those groups at one time or another. When I belonged to the last group, I found myself divorced after 16 years of marriage when my girls were seven and nine. This changed my life forever. I became a single mother and so was on call 24 hours a day. I decided to go back to college and get a teaching degree which was probably the most positive decision I could have made.

In trying to balance my family life while going to school and working, I needed to consider how to balance the needs of my children. Children always need us – only in different ways at different times. You might have children of various ages like the woman I once talked with who had seven children. She said that if you must leave them, do it when they are young because they really need you when they hit the teen years. Yes, the turbulent teen years, when you might get the best chance to talk with them as they come home from school in the afternoon. Unfortunately, I was not able to be home during the day in my children's teen years, but we were still able to stay connected by cell phone after work. I went to their soccer games and swim meets and spent as much time as possible with them. Here are a few more ideas to help carve out time with your family:

1. Dinner at Home Night:
    Pick one night a week where everyone is required to be home for dinner. This is a great way to teach them to cook, encourage conversation, and develop family unity.

2. Stay at Home Day:
    We declared a Stay at Home Day on the weekends periodically, and the kids loved it. No one was allowed to go anywhere, except for me if we needed food. This may involve saying "No" to some activities, but the payoff is that there is no pressure to go anywhere and you get sustained time together.

3. Church at Home?
    Yes, I believe it is important to attend spiritual services. However, some Sundays we stayed at home and had our own services. We would sing together as I played the piano. We would read scripture passages and pray together. This time is especially nice if you have younger children because they enjoy the personal attention.

4. Special events with Individual Children:
    If you know that your child has a special interest in a subject or a particular person, see if you can arrange to go to an event together. Whether it is in music, theater, sports, or dinner at a favorite restaurant, your child will remember these times together forever! They will be so excited to have you all to themselves!

5. Use the Internet to Your Advantage:
    Many children are so connected that many times we want them to take time away from their devices. You may be able to have fun by picking a game that you both can play over time like Words with Friends that is similar to Scrabble. Check out this article for five more games that you can play together called Five Incredibly Addictive Mindbending Online Games found at Goodnet (http://www.goodnet.org/articles/5-incredibly-addictive-mindbending-online-games?utm_source=goodnet-site&utm_medium=footer-related&utm_campaign=goodnet-related).
    They include 100 Most Common English Words, TypeRacer, Online Color Challenge, Geoguesser, and The Great Language Game.

When you are looking for balance, you may decide that staying home with your children full-time or part-time seems right for you. You may still need income to accomplish this, so you would have to consider alternative ways to work at home.

Here are a few ways to think about:

1. Job share with someone or work part-time so that your hours are in the morning and you will be home with the children after school.

2. Take a look at SideHustleNation.com
    www.sidehustlenation.com for many part-time opportunities that you may not have heard of or thought

CHAPTER 4

Starting Your Own Business

I Want to Do What I Want to Do!

Are you tired of working for someone else and wanting to work for yourself? Congratulations! You are embarking on an exciting journey. The best way to do this without burning out or failing fast is to have a great business plan. One of the best places to get help with a business plan is an organization called SCORE. Retired business executives who serve as free mentors are there to help guide you along with workshops and great business information to get you started right. It is important to have a business plan, and you will find great information at the Small Business Administration at www.sba.gov as well as SCORE. Here you will find business advice along with options for business loans of various types.

Here is a quote about how large this organization is:

"With over 10,000 volunteers in more than 300 chapters across the nation offering expertise in over 62 industries, we have the knowledge and tools you need to reach your business goals."

Please refer to Chapter 15 for ten key steps to starting your own business, along with people who can give you great information. After reviewing your business plan, you will need to weigh all of the financial factors as well as your personal and family obligations.

A big part of success in helping you fulfill your obligations is to build a team of professionals that can help you with legal, accounting, banking, technology, and marketing assistance. You may not need them full-time, but finding people who can give you this assistance will be a great asset to you.

By using your networking skills, you will increase your chances of finding the right people by listening to other business owners in your community. You can find them at your local Chamber of Commerce, Meetups where business leaders congregate, or trusted friends and associates.

Look for books by people who are in the same field that you are expanding or exploring and see what insight you can find from them. When you mix all of your knowledge and focus on your vision, you will need to develop your unique brand.

In today's economy, YOU are your brand. Your product or service is secondary to the story of how you have come to present your ideas to your customers.

Storytelling is an important part of getting people to understand you and your message. People become engaged and interested by listening to your story which is a big part of your brand. I highly recommend Michael Margolis and his message at GetStoried.com if you need help crafting your own story in a compelling way.

> Your brand is your reputation—the perception of you held by the external world. Your brand is the unique combination of personal attributes, values, drivers, strengths, and passions that define you. Your brand helps those assessing you determine whether they should hire you or do business with you.

> – Meg Guiseppi, www.executiveresumebranding.com

From *Social Networking for Career Success* by Miriam Salpeter.

These are important questions that I have learned to ask before going into business for yourself:

What are your purpose and vision?

What are your goals and values?

What do you want for your life in one year? 3 years? 5 years?

What are your strengths and weaknesses?

What will differentiate you from your competition?

What are the needs of the people in your target market and how will you deliver what people want?

There are many resources to help you in Chapter 15.

Before you begin planning your new business, go to the Wheel of Life exercise in Chapter 6, Part II to get clarity on where you are now, then make goals on the Personal Goals Worksheet which will help shape the future for the beginning of your new business.

RESOURCES

Margolis, Michael. www.getstoried.com

Guiseppi, Meg. www.executiveresumebranding.com

Salpeter, Miriam. (2013). Social Networking for Career Success.

Learning Express

SCORE. www.score.org

Small Business Administration. www.sba.gov

CHAPTER 5

Balancing Retirement With Work

A New Way to Work

Retirement planning can be interesting because you never know what kind of situation you may find yourself in. First, assess how much money you'll need to support yourself in the future. The Association of Retired Persons (AARP) has a tool that you can use to see if you are saving enough at http://www.aarp.org/work/retirement-planning/retirement_calculator.html
Suze Orman has many retirement resources available on her site as well.

Figuring out your retirement planning will take into consideration all of your sources of income including savings, Social Security, investments, and real estate properties.

Keep up with Social Security Changes

Some good things to know regarding Social Security benefits:
- If you work until full retirement age, there will be no reduction in your Social Security benefits for any work that you do.

- If you are collecting Social Security retirement benefits before full retirement age, your benefits are reduced by $1 for every $2 you earn over the limit. For the year 2016, this limit on earned income is $15,720 ($1,310 per month). The amount goes up each year.

- In determining whether to either postpone your retirement or cut back on your work hours, call the Social Security Administration at (800) 772-1213 or use the SSA Retirement Estimator. The SSA can tell you exactly what your benefits will be under different scenarios. The Social Security picture will no doubt continue to change which is why it is more important than ever to get your income sources up and running.

- You should remember to sign up for Medicare at age 65. The window of time you have to do this begins three months before your 65th birthday and ends three months afterward.

Take a look at your budget and determine how much money you need to live on or how much would give you a comfortable monthly boost. Think about how much you would like to set aside for an extra vacation or something that really excites you!

If you have had an average income and not much money saved for retirement, here is a chance to dream about what you really want to do and find a way to do it to supplement the social security check you will be getting. You may have decided to retire early, be part of a retiring couple, or be living alone and find that you need some extra income.

The good news is that by this time you have lived long enough and paid attention, so you have some valuable wisdom to offer other people. You may want to consider consulting or teaching a class, using your crafting skills, writing a book, or working part-time in a place that you consider fun and motivational.

Have Fun and Get Paid

Did you know that you can get paid to travel if that is what you want to do? Explore the options here at 10 Jobs That Pay You to Travel at Abroad.com. (http://theabroadguide.com/10-jobs-that-pay-you-to-travel) There are links in this article to places where you can become certified to teach English because one of the options is to teach English in a foreign country.

Have you ever thought about doing a side job to earn a few extra dollars or pay an unexpected bill? SideHustleNation.com is a site dedicated to part-time jobs that make extra income. When you go to this site and look around, there is a list of 99 jobs in a blog post that you can browse to get you thinking.

Maybe you have been in charge of a corporation, and you are ready to manage some other kind of organization. There may be a local non-profit that you are passionate about that would hire you to work with them. Former President, Jimmy Carter, continues to make a difference for people by working with Habitat for Humanity in his nineties. Check your city for opportunities in the areas that interest you.

Volunteer Opportunities that Save You Money

Theater tickets can be very expensive. If you are a lover of theater and drama, contact your local theater and see if they have a program for volunteer ushers. We have one here in Seattle, Washington, at the Paramount Theater. That way you can get to see your favorite shows without breaking your budget.

Whether you would like to travel near or far, becoming a house sitter could save you a considerable amount of money. House sitters agree to take care of a person's home and property in exchange for a place to live for a specific amount of time. Housecarers.com, in business since 2000, helps make secure matches between house owners and house sitters.

Living Cheaply Abroad and in the USA

If you have a dream of living in a foreign country, you might be able to finance your lifestyle by using the Internet for virtual consulting, teaching, or selling photography. You may want to consider starting a business in the local economy where you want to live.

There are less expensive places to live in the world and here is how to find them. If you want to live in a foreign country for part of the year, you can find inexpensive places to compare at the Cheapest Destinations Blog (www.cheapestdestinationsblog.com). If you are interested in moving to a great place in the United States, you can research and compare your favorite places on Livability.com.

These truly can be the best days of your life while living on your Social Security check. When you are making your plans, be sure to give some thought to your health.

Consider Your Health

The cost of health care seems to be out of control for many these days. Even with Medicare, you have to pay for supplemental insurance to pick up the difference of the bill that Medicare doesn't pay in your retirement years. It does pay to consider your health to be of paramount importance, with attention to nutritious meals and exercise. Addressing and managing any health issues with your health care providers will help keep you in the best shape and frame of mind to enjoy your retirement.

My father just turned 80 this September. He walks every day and is in great shape because he has built his lifestyle around that over the years. Just going outside and walking around the block to start is a great idea.

There are many ways to make fitness fun. Whatever you consider playing is a great place to start. Do you dance or swim? Walking is one of the best ways to exercise. Make dates on your calendar to visit local parks and get outside to get fresh air. Find a partner to walk with or join in whatever you consider to be play. Since taking care of your health is one of the most important parts of retirement, find what works best for you and take action to make it happen, so you will be able to enjoy the people and events that matter most to you.

Now go to the Wheel of Life in Chapter 6, Part II to gauge where you are now and use the Personal Goals Worksheet to help you make some goals that will propel you toward an enjoyable retirement.

RESOURCES

AARP. www.aarp.org

Cheapest Destinations Blog. www.cheapestdestinationsblog.com

Housecarers.com. www.housecarers.com

Livability. www.livability.com

Orman, Suze. www.suzeorman.com

Side Hustle Nation. www.sidehustlenation.com

Social Security Administration. www.ssa.gov

Also, check your local listings for an office near you.

PART TWO

Connect with Your Joy and Choose a Path That Excites You!

CHAPTER 6

Take Stock of Where You Are Now

Reflect on Your Current Path

Before you continue on the path of reconnecting with your joy, it is a good idea to take some time to reflect on where you are right now. The different areas of our lives are constantly changing and so are our goals. Some of you may be at the end of raising children and see the empty nest coming. Others are more focused on getting their retirement plans in place soon.

The Wheel of Life Worksheet will give you clarity on where you are now and then the Personal Goals Worksheet will help you think about making goals to achieve the balance you want. I'd suggest evaluating about every six months to keep you in touch with what you really want out of life.

Use the Wheel of Life worksheet below to take a few minutes to rate the various parts of your life on a scale from 1 to 10. Read the descriptions, and rate each according to where you are now. This will give you a snapshot of where you are in your life balance right now. What did you find out? What areas do you feel you want to work on? Is there anything that stands out to you?

The dots that are closer to the center will be the areas that need more work. If your circle is fairly uniform, but there is one point that stands out above the rest, you probably are the most balanced in that area. If most of your circle is toward the outer edges and you have one or two areas that show below it, these would be the areas that need the most balance. Put a date on it and review it at least every six months to evaluate the progress you are making with your life balance.

After you have looked over your Wheel of Life, use the Personal Goals Worksheet to make goals in any areas you want to change.

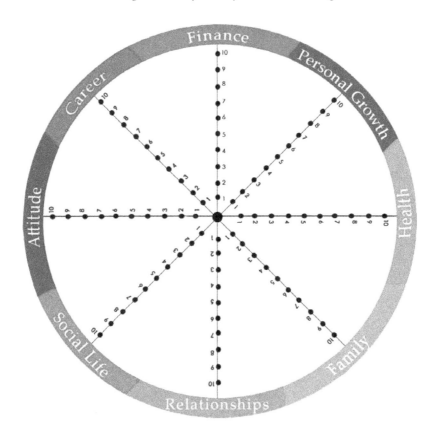

Explanation of each section with goals to consider:

Finances

This is not about how much you have but rather how you relate to money. There are some millionaires who worry themselves sick about money and so might score very low here and others who have just enough to get by and simply go with the flow.

A 10 is someone totally at ease with money whereas a 1 is someone so worried about money all the time and it is causing them great stress.

Goals:

Set up a regular savings plan.
Use a budget to plan spending.
Contribute to an emergency fund.
Save for a specific purpose such as a house or car.

Personal Growth

Successful people commit themselves continually to learning and improving themselves. Are you a 10 – committed to learning as much as you can about life by constantly experiencing new opportunities? Do you regularly read to learn and grow so you can stretch and improve yourself? Since you are reading this, you are certainly not a 1 or a 2.

Goals:

Read on a regular basis.
Attend a conference related to your personal growth.
Find and/or meet with a mentor.

Health

We all take our health for granted until we are not feeling well. How is yours? Do you look after yourself by eating well and regularly exercising? Having a long-term illness does not necessarily mean you need to give yourself a low score. The main thing is whether you are doing all you can to improve or regulate your condition.

Goals:

Commit to one simple change at a time.
Establish exercise or play time on your calendar.
Make time to de-stress during your day.

Family

Family life is very important. Although family life should be loving, caring and supportive, it often is not for a variety of reasons such as crying babies, wild teenage sons or daughters, or constant arguments and tensions. These situations can be a huge challenge and affect other areas of your life including work, studies, and relationships. Family life could mean just your immediate family or a more extended family. Whatever family life means to you, give yourself a current score.

Goals:

Plan family time together at least once a week.
Attend a special event with one of your children at a time.
Visit or contact extended family to keep in touch.

Relationships

Consider the key relationship you have whether it is with your boyfriend/girlfriend husband/wife/friend or family member. Where do you feel it is at? Where would you like it to be?

Goals:

Spend time with your loved one that is meaningful to both of you.
Go on a date.
Plan time to communicate your plans and dreams.
Do something special for your loved one.

Social Life

This can be about the quality of your social life which can score very low for people with busy careers. However, you can also decide to score it based on how you interact with people and how often you get to socialize. A vital component of life is the need to interact with people. How comfortable are you are in social situations? Some people are the life and soul of every party and some will not want to speak up when there is a group of people around. Give yourself a score.

Goals:

Invite friends over to your house or go out with them for coffee, lunch, or dinner.
Get to know people in your neighborhood.
Volunteer in your community for a cause that is important to you.

PERSONAL GOALS WORKSHEET

HEALTH

I will_____

by_____.

One thing I will do this week to work toward my goal is

_____.

PERSONAL GROWTH

I will_____

by_____.

One thing I will do this week to work toward my goal is

_____.

FINANCE

I will_____

by_____.

One thing I will do this week to work toward my goal is

_____.

ATTITUDE

I will_____

by_____.

One thing I will do this week to work toward my goal is

_____.

SOCIAL LIFE

I will_____

by_____.

One thing I will do this week to work toward my goal is

_____.

FAMILY

I will_____

by_____.

One thing I will do this week to work toward my goal is

_____.

RELATIONSHIPS

I will_____

by_____.

One thing I will do this week to work toward my goal is

_____.

CAREER

I will_____

by_____.

One thing I will do this week to work toward my goal is

_____.

CHAPTER 7

Make a Mind Shift

People are about as happy as they make their minds up to be. – Abraham Lincoln

After taking a look at your life balance using the Wheel of Life and Personal Goals Worksheet, you may decide that you definitely want to change your current career path. You might decide you want to move in a different direction in your current job or leave the company where you are altogether. Before you make a decision, I want you to evaluate your thinking.

If you are unhappy, frustrated, or depressed for any reason, you are not in a good place to decide what your next career step should be. It is understandable that you might feel this way because there seems to be no opportunity for advancement in your current job. You may be stuck at home, and the situation is wearing on you. You have the opportunity to go in the opposite direction by changing your perspective and commitment.

Debbie Desy worked in corporate America for people whom she felt did not appreciate her work. The situation became tedious and frustrating. She began to think about what she really wanted to do. Debbie had always been interested in becoming a massage therapist. She stopped into a school to see what the coursework would be like.

After becoming very intrigued, her next step was to enroll in night classes while still working at her current job. Upon graduation, Debbie started her own massage therapy practice in a downtown building in

Everett, Washington. She made a plan to move her practice to her home within five years. She now has a beautiful massage studio attached to her home.

If she had decided that there was no way out of her frustrating job, she would still be stifled and not able to use her talents and strengths. You can visit Debbie on Facebook at "The Earth Cocoon Wellness Massage."

If you do not have any dreams, the reason might be that your supply of joy has run dry. I want to encourage you to awaken that part of you that hasn't laughed in several months...or maybe years. If your job is depriving you of living joyfully, then reframe your thinking a bit.

Think about this scenario: People are paying you money to follow your dreams. You have the financial security from your current job to seek out better options. Revel in the knowledge that this job is not your permanent working place. Determine to make a plan to find out what you are passionate about and go in that direction. It may take you some time, so think of your current position as a bonus.

Your productivity at work may improve because you see the light at the end of the tunnel. Do your best; you may need that recommendation from your boss. Maybe you are looking for a promotion, and you will get one. If you are changing careers, you will have time to do it in an orderly fashion and have the funds to do it. These transitions usually don't happen overnight.

We are living in a global community, more and more every day. This means the opportunities for you are endless. We are held back by our own beliefs of what we can and cannot do. My grandma used to say, "Find a need and fill it." If you do this in our present day economy, you will not lack in abundance.

If you feel that there are serious blocks to your moving ahead, I recommend *The Artist's Way* by Julia Cameron. This book encourages you to write the Morning Pages, a journaling exercise where you set aside a certain amount of time each morning to write everything that comes to your mind so that you can get past the issues that are holding you back. She lays out a series of exercises that help you move past blocks to your creativity.

The difference between moving ahead and staying stuck is about what is going on inside your mind. Move ahead as if you cannot fail. You may have to pivot in a different direction on your way to the goal, but if you keep taking positive steps you will get there.

Let's move on to Chapter 8 and visualize your dreams.

RESOURCES

Canfield, Jack (2015). *The Success Principles: How to Get from Where You Are to Where You Want to Be.* William Morrow Paperbacks
The book is packed full of great advice, and there is also a free 10-day course at www.jackcanfield.com. When you implement these principles, you will have a great foundation for success.

Cameron, Julia (2016). *The Artist's Way – 25th Anniversary Edition.* Tarcher Perigree

Desy, Debbie. The Earth Cocoon Wellness Massage, Facebook

Eggen, John (2004). *Create the Business Breakthrough You Want: Secrets and Strategies from the World's Greatest Mentors.* Mission Publishing
Advice from over 50 great mentors including pages of great advice on Business Strategy, Leadership Development, Marketing & Sales, Personal Growth, and Wealth Building.

Ferriss, Timothy (2009). *The 4-Hour Workweek: Escape 9-5, Live Anywhere, and Join the New Rich.* New York: Crown Publishers
www.tim.blog

Ferriss started out talking about working less and having more freedom beginning in 2007. He introduced the topic of the New Rich. People who were not chained to their desks but could live a great life. He uses this quote in his book:

"One does not accumulate but eliminate. It is not daily increase but daily decrease. The height of cultivation always runs to simplicity." – Bruce Lee

There are some great mindset shifts in this book.
He has also just released *Tools of Titans.*

Ferriss, Timothy (2016). *Tools of Titans: The Tactics, Routines, and Habits of Billionaires, Icons, and World-Class Performers* . Houghton Mifflin Harcourt
This book is a compilation of his many podcasts and the wisdom he has gained over the years.

Hyatt, Michael. www.MichaelHyatt.com

Michael Hyatt is a virtual business mentor who writes about reaching your potential, becoming more productive, building your team, and building your influence. He has many resources on his web site and is also an author.

Shipman, Claire and Katty Kay (2009). *Womenomics* . New York: Harper Collins
These women did research on women in the workplace and found that
"It turns out that women are incredibly valuable and inconveniently expensive to replace."
As women, we already know this, but it could help you when negotiations draw near. Women are incredibly good at building a network of colleagues to support them both in their current positions and when they

move to a different company. Men are not as resourceful when they move.

Vitale, Joe (2010). *Attract Money Now*. Hypnotic Marketing, Inc.

Joe was once homeless, and now he makes a great amount of money. He talks about how our beliefs about money are limiting our income. It is an interesting read which is full of insight. You can purchase the Kindle edition for just 99 cents.

CHAPTER 8

Visualize Your Dreams

Some days I have thought of six impossible things before breakfast. -Lewis Carroll

In this chapter, you will explore how you would like your life to be. The Dream Weaver worksheet is on the next page. The purpose of this page is to get you to do some dreaming about your future.

Don't hold anything back, just write it all down. Be very specific. Once you have written down your goals, I want you to imagine exactly how you would feel if you had already achieved them. Let that feeling sink in. If you want financial freedom, think about why and what you would be able to accomplish. Who would you be able to help? Where would you travel? Maybe you just want to stay home and work from there. Write it all down and savor it.

The reason athletes use visualization techniques is because they are so powerful. If you can see and feel what you would like to accomplish, and think about it with excitement, your subconscious mind will steer you in the right direction. Like a computer, your mind will help get you where you need to go.

Your subconscious mind cannot tell the difference between your imagination and what is real. That is why visualization techniques work so well.

Read about the research at Harvard here: http://drdavidhamilton.com/visualisation-alters-the-brain-body/. You may find that you will want to do another Dream Weaver Worksheet after you have worked through this program. Life is a process, and there is something very powerful about writing down your goals and dreams with a pen and paper.

After you are done visualizing and writing down what you want for your life, move on to Chapter 9 where we will look at your Points of Joy.

DREAM WEAVER WORKSHEET

Here you are going to do some dreaming about what you would like your life to be like in the future. Be specific about what you will be able to have and to do in this next phase of your life.

What is your idea of a dream career right now? Think about your core values and how they fit into what you want to do. What are the main goals that you will be able to accomplish?

_____

_____

_____

_____

What does your daily and weekly schedule look like? Will you have more time for your family? What specifically will you be able to do with them or for them? Will you travel?

Be very specific in your dreams and goals.

_____

_____

_____

_____

_____

_____

_____

_____

_____

Be sure to write all of your goals and dreams down. Use another sheet of paper if you need to.

VERY IMPORTANT:

After you have your goals and dreams written down, take a few minutes to imagine that each one of your goals and dreams has been achieved. How do you feel? The stronger you feel, the more your subconscious mind will help propel you in that direction. Put your goals and dreams on 3 x 5 index cards and refer to them at least once every day to help you stay motivated and moving in the direction you want. The more you can visualize and feel what it is like to have already accomplished what you desire, the more effective your efforts will be.

Make a Vision Board

To further help you visualize your dreams, I recommend making a Vision Board. You can make one with poster board, a thin cardboard sheet that you find at your local office supply store. You will also need magazines, pictures, markers, scissors, and glue or tape. Find pictures that represent what you want for your future and put them on the board, so you will be able to see them every day. There are also online vision board programs that will help you make one for your iPhone or tablet. Another way to make a Vision Board is to make a board on Pinterest.com with pictures of what you desire.

You can also make an Affirmation Board in much the same way with quotes and sayings that will help motivate and inspire you. You can go to www.makeavisionboard.com and find 100 positive affirmations along with several choices for vision board software.

When you think about your goals and dreams and write them down, you are much more likely to achieve them. This is crucial because you will move in the direction of wherever you focus your attention.

RESOURCES

Hamilton, Dr. David H. "Visualisation Alters the Brain and Body" Web.

19 April 2011
http://drdavidhamilton.com/visualisation-alters-the-brain-body/

Make a Vision Board.com. www.makeavisionboard.com

CHAPTER 9

Define Your Points of Joy

Find joy in the journey. -Thomas S. Monson

Think back to the most exciting times in your life? What were they? How did you feel? What if you could experience that feeling every day without much effort? If you are doing something you love, it is more like having candy than a career. What would you love to do that would make you bound out of bed in the morning? It gets you so excited that it's hard for you to sleep at night, it's kind of like falling in love. Now that, my friend, is living, not merely existing, and that is what I want for you.

Go to the Points of Joy Worksheet at the end of this chapter. Start with your earliest memories, write down your memories of what brought you joy and you were so excited about doing it, you lost track of time, or were in a "state of flow." You might find that the things you loved as a child are still the thoughts you treasure today.

Here is an example using some of my Points of Joy and how they affect me today. I have loved reading books all my life. One of my favorite experiences is when my elementary school librarian had me read poems on tape and send them to the author, Thelma Evelyn Jones. She wrote a letter back and sent an autographed copy of her book which I still treasure today. My love of reading led to a degree in teaching. I love teaching children, and now I am writing books.

Completing professional life coach certification fulfilled a dream of mine to find a framework to help women like me who are craving change in their career lives. Writing this book is an extension of that dream.

When you have written down all your points of joy, it is time to look for the themes of your life in Chapter 10.

Points of Joy

Record times when you felt joy. Whether it was music, sports, or just a special moment that inspired you, record it here. Pay attention to any time where you felt a "state of flow" at school, work, or play.

CHILDHOOD

_____

_____

_____

_____

_____

TEEN YEARS

_____

_____

_____

_____

_____

TWENTIES

_____

_____

_____

_____

_____

THIRTIES

_____

_____

_____

_____

_____

FORTIES

_____

_____

_____

_____

_____

FIFTIES

_____

_____

_____

_____

_____

SIXTIES

_____

_____

_____

_____

_____

PRESENT DAY

_____

_____

_____

_____

_____

CHAPTER 10

Find the Themes of Your Life

I am a part of all I have met. -Alfred Lord Tennyson

Look over your Points of Joy and discover patterns of behavior that reveal personal characteristics that you can see from your earliest memories and write them down.

For example, if you always loved music, numbers, or exercise, chances are you still love activities that include those now. If you loved giving attention to senior citizens, children, or pets, you might find yourself in a place that involves activities that cater to your interests. When you begin to think about the themes you see, that is part of what makes you connect with your joy. In the next section, you will work on clarifying your strengths and then later see where these themes of your life intersect with them.

Themes of My Life

Record patterns that you find in your behavior that reveal personal characteristics along with experiences that require similar thinking or skills you find from your Points of Joy worksheet.

PERSONAL CHARACTERISTICS

_____

_____

_____

_____

_____

_____

THINKING PROCESSES OR SKILLS THAT YOU
FIND IN YOUR EXPERIENCES

_____

_____

_____

_____

_____

_____

HOW DO THE THEMES IN YOUR LIFE COMPARE TO WHAT YOU ARE DOING NOW?

_____

_____

_____

_____

_____

_____

Let's move on to Chapter 11 where we work on emphasizing your strengths.

Emphasize Your Strengths

Everything nourishes what is strong already.
—Jane Austen

Many times when we are called in for a job review, we hear about our weaknesses and make plans to improve them. Your strongest weakness will never equal your weakest strength.

We are made with certain inherent strengths in areas where we will naturally excel. Another word for your strengths would be capabilities. Why not focus on those areas and choose careers where you can use them the best?

Long hours working in an area of our work that does not come naturally to us can make us physically sick. When you are doing a task or work that does not come naturally to you, this causes you to struggle to get it done. When you struggle, you don't enjoy your work, and this causes you stress and frustration. You owe it to your health and happiness to find your strengths and use them in a way where you can thrive.

Think about your current work and see where you are using your strengths. Maybe you can delegate work that is not in your strongest area to someone on your team or an assistant so you can focus on what you do best. Would a shift to a different department be better for you? Does the thought of extra training appeal to you so you can be working in an area of strength? When you have thought through all the options, it may be possible that your current job simply can't make the most of your strengths.

One efficient way to determine your strengths is to take an inventory or assessment of them. On the next page, decide on which strength assessments you would like to take and then fill out the Finding My Strengths Worksheet.

Finding My Strengths

Use at least one of the following methods to find or confirm your strengths.

StrengthsFinder 2.0 is a book by Tom Rath that has a code you can use to take an online assessment. Tom Rath has based his book on the work of Donald O. Clifton, Ph.D. who is considered the Father of Strengths-Based Psychology. The assessment helps you find your natural talents and gives ideas on how you can develop and use them to your best advantage. Learn more at www.strengthsfinder.com.

Richard Step /Free Strengths and Weaknesses Aptitude Test
http://richardstep.com/richardstep-strengths-weaknesses-aptitude-test

LIST YOUR TOP FIVE STRENGTHS ACCORDING TO THE ASSESSMENT YOU TOOK:

1. _____

2. _____

3. _____

4. _____

5. _____

HOW ARE YOU USING YOUR STRENGTHS RIGHT NOW?

_____

_____

_____

HOW WOULD YOU LIKE TO USE THEM IN THE FUTURE?

_____

_____

_____

RESOURCES

Rath, Tom (2007). *StrengthsFinder 2.0*. New York: Gallup Press

Use the individualized code that comes with the book for an online assessment that will show you your top five strengths. The book will tell you about those strengths, ideas for action, and how to work with people who have the 34 themes of strength that are listed.

You can also go to the website at www.strengthsfinder.com and purchase a Top Five Strength assessment for $15.00.

Step, Richard – Free Online Strengths and Weakness Aptitude Test

http://richardstep.com/richardstep-strengths-weaknesses-aptitude-test.

CHAPTER 12

What Are Your Options?

It's time to start living the life you've imagined.
-Henry James

Once you've figured out your strengths, think about what brings you joy and see where they intersect. What career move would you like to make? If you are not sure, there are some great career assessments that you may want to consider. A career assessment is a tool you can use to evaluate your traits to see what career might be the best for you. Take a look at the suggestions for career assessments on the worksheet below.

After you have filled out your top five career choices from the assessments you took, consider how what brings you joy and your strengths blend together best. Go immediately to Chapter 13 to consider your choices and write out a plan for action.

Chapter 14 will show you some examples of what is possible when you start in a new direction. Part III will give you resources and valuable information on various paths to success.

CAREER ASSESSMENTS

Here are my suggestions for career assessments.

Please go to a site called www.humanmetrics.com and click on the upper left-hand corner where it says Jung Typology Test and Jung Career Indicator and take that test. This is known as the Myers-Briggs Test. It will show how your personality is suited for various careers. Even if you have taken this test before, you may find out some additional information, because our interests can change over time.

Minnesota State has developed a career resource section, and they offer various free assessments at https://www.careerwise.mnscu.edu/careers/assessyourself.html. They also have other resources to help with your career search.

If you are in need of very detailed information, the last resource I recommend is located at www.assessment.com. It is called the MAPP assessment, and it is very thorough and will give you insight into many areas of your life as they relate to a career choice. You can take it for free and get basic information and then if you want in-depth results, you will have to pay for those.

Take a look at what you find out and think about what area you may want to pursue as you go into the future.

PLEASE LIST YOUR TOP FIVE CAREER CHOICES:

_____

_____

_____

_____

_____

CAREER RESOURCES

Jung Typology Test and Jung Career Indicator (known as the Myers-Briggs Test). www.humanmetrics.com.

MAPP Assessment. www.assessment.com.

Minnesota State

www.careerwise.mnscu.edu/careers/assessyourself.html.

CHAPTER 13

Get a TAN (Take Action Now) Where Do I Go From Here?

Boldness has genius, magic, and power in it. Begin it now. -Goethe

How exciting! You have looked at your points of joy, your strengths and taken a career assessment. What have you found? Now you are at the point where you can really consider the direction you would like to take. Think about what brings you joy, combine that with your strengths, and match that with a career choice from the assessment you took. What does that look like? Do you want to follow that course of action or is there a variation that suits you better?

Which of the following direction or directions have you decided to pursue?

*Stay at your current position only move in a different direction.

*Look for a different position with another company.

* Go back to school to get the skills to achieve the results you want.

* Start your own company

* Write a book or several books

* Do consulting, teaching, or speaking, in your field of expertise.

Please write out your plan on the following lines. Take a look at the resources at the end of this chapter and then go to PART III for further help with your chosen path.

_____

_____

_____

_____

_____

_____

_____

_____

_____

_____

_____

_____

_____

_____

_____

_____

_____

_____

_____

_____

_____

_____

_____

_____

_____

_____

_____

_____

_____

_____

_____

RESOURCES

Local newspaper and online employment sections in areas that you would like to work.

Andres, Patricia A. and Eleanor A. Hill (2013). *Win the Job You Want! 7 Secrets Hiring Managers Don't Tell You, But We Will!* HigherLife Publishing and Marketing

Blake, Jenny. (2016). *Pivot: The Only Move That Matters Is Your Next One.* New York: Portfolio/Penguin. www.pivotmethod.com

Jenny gives practical advice on how to navigate your current career situation, whether you want upward mobility where you are now or you want to launch out in a different career direction.

Block, Jay A. (2010). *101 Best Ways to Land a Job in Troubled Times.* McGraw-Hill

Practical advice on job searching in a time when jobs are hard to find. Jay talks about having a positive mindset as you search for your next job opportunity as evidenced by this quote. Jay says:

> "If you face your adversities in a courageous and positive manner, you can make the best of any circumstance. The bottom line is that you have the power to control how you feel at any moment, no matter what the situation."

When something upsets you, shift your focus and move on.

Bolles, Richard N. (2017) *What Color is Your Parachute?: A Practical Manual for Job-Hunters and Career-Changers.* New York: Ten Speed Press/Random House, Inc.
Updated annually, there is a great deal of career changing advice here. This book is a classic in the job hunting world.

Kay, Andrea (2013). *This is How to Get Your Next Job: An Inside Look at What Employers Really Want.* New York: AMACON

Kay says:

> "Every company is hiring people who can offer precisely what they need when they need it." Find out what the company you want to work for needs and offer it to them.

LinkedIn. www.linkedin.com. See Chapter 14 for a detailed description.

The Muse. www.themuse.com.

This web site has up to date information on the culture for different companies and also lists job openings for careers in major American cities. There are many interesting articles related to searching for a career that may appeal to you. You can subscribe to their newsletter as well.

Scudamore, Patricia and Hilton Catt (2012). *Successful Job Hunting In a Week.* London: Hodder Education/A Hachette UK Company
Save time and learn important job-hunting skills such as finding the right job for you and deciding which job offers to accept.

Sullivan, Maya (2015). *Dare to Be Your Own Boss: Follow Your Passion, Create a Niche.* Synergy Books. www.mayasullivan.com
Search here for an overview of many different kinds of businesses you may be interested in. The book has a tool that allows you to compare your choices in an online format. Find resources here to help you make a good impression when you go to an interview.

PART THREE

Maps for Your Journey

CHAPTER 14

Networking

Networking is vital to your career research as you never know who you will meet that might be the one to give you an opportunity that is related to your career advancement.

Networking also provides a way to find out about the culture of the prospective companies you would like to consider for your next career move. As you know, the people that you work with every day are a big indicator of how positive your work environment will be.

If you can find out about the people who you will be working with directly, that would be a big help to you. Before an interview, go online to research the prospective company on their company web site for information about company culture and also do a search on Google for that company name to see what comes up. After an interview where you have met your prospective colleagues and manager, research on LinkedIn to see what the background of the people you will be working with is like. Pay attention to articles they have written. If you know someone who also works for that company, talk to them about their experience as well.

You will find networking to be one of the most valuable strategies in your job search and also especially if you are starting your own business. Pay attention to all of the people you meet. They are all a part of your network. Networking is not about collecting as many business cards as possible; it is about building meaningful relationships over time.

I highly recommend the book *Never Eat Alone* by Keith Ferrazzi, on building relationships.

> Take all of your new contacts, all that data, and take action. Establish communities of passion, and create opportunities for collaboration. Gather up all those smart people in a process of simultaneous learning and doing. Create or join projects that involve important segments of your network…

–Keith Ferrazzi

Think of ways that you can be helpful. Look for ways to work together that will be mutually beneficial. Good networking involves you surrounding yourself with the kind of people who have access or influence in the places you want to go and the things you want to do. If you would like to approach someone, find a way to be helpful to them first. When you are looking for your new career or newly formed business, it makes sense to find groups of people who are interested in what you have to offer. LinkedIn is one of the best places to connect with recruiters and online groups of people in your chosen field. You can also explore companies where you would like to work.

LINKEDIN

LinkedIn is a huge database of information and a great place to find out about companies that interest you.

When you type in the name of a company, you can find job listings, people who work for the company, and groups where people from that company participate. This way you can build relationships and network with your specific career goal in mind. The people you connect with will be able to access information about you when you have filled out a LinkedIn profile. You will also be able to send direct messages to people you would like to contact.

In order to get the maximum success, fill out your profile as completely as possible. In the summary, give the precise description of what it is that you can offer to your customers/clients. I help _____ (your target market) to _____ (the outcome you provide).

Find groups of people that are discussing the field you are interested in and join in the conversation. Begin networking by adding helpful value to the discussion. If there is anything that you want to do, chances are someone has already successfully achieved it. Go find the people who are successful and see what they are doing.

You can convert the URL address that LinkedIn gives your profile to have your name included in that URL for LinkedIn. It's easy now, since they changed their format. Go to your home page and click on edit public profile. You will see a place on the right to edit your URL. The format is: http://www.linkedin./in/yourname. Now you can use the new URL for your business cards and other branding.

VOLUNTEERING

Volunteering is one of the best ways to connect with people. Choose activities that you are interested in where there are the kind of people you are trying to meet. For instance, companies participate in many charitable events. You could find one that pertains to the particular company you are looking into that appeals to your interests. There are food drives, health initiatives, runs for various causes, hospital campaigns to help a certain group of patients, literacy events to supply books to low-income families and schools, and much more.

NETWORKING ON A NATIONAL AND REGIONAL LEVEL

There are associations and organizations who hold conferences all around the country pertaining to many different topics and career fields. Consider attending one to invest in your professional growth and extend your network. Find a conference that invites the kind of people who you need to meet or work with. Many joint ventures are formed at these events.

A joint venture is a mutually beneficial agreement between two parties. This could be for cross promotion or one-sided promotion of products or services to your audiences. Maybe you will work together on a project or host a webinar together. Before asking something from a prospective joint venture partner, find a way to be helpful to them. See if you are a good fit for their audience because you have something valuable to offer them that they would want.

NETWORKING IN YOUR CITY

In addition to associations and organizations, there are Meetup groups for every kind of interest. Local Meetup groups in your area can also be great ways to connect with people. You can go to www.Meetup.com and find one near you or even start one of your own.

YOUR PERSONAL SPHERE OF INFLUENCE

Trust, credibility, authority, and resources are all important to getting your message out. You want to start with warm calls first. Look at the people you know and begin to contact them. They may be able to give you referrals if they are not interested themselves.

You would be surprised how large your actual network is. If you haven't already started, use the Who Do You Know form on the next page to help you. It is much easier to contact people you already know.

CREATE A SYSTEM

Have a system to keep track of the people you meet. In the beginning, if all you do is keep an Excel spreadsheet with information about your contacts, the date you spoke to them, and what you spoke to them about, that will give a big boost to managing your relationships.

Check out ACT, Salesforce, or any Customer Relationship Management system that appeals to you. You need a way to track your relationships.

Who Do You Know?

Family

_____
_____
_____
_____
_____
_____
_____

Friends

_____
_____
_____
_____
_____
_____

Organizations & Associations

_____
_____
_____
_____
_____

School

_____
_____
_____
_____
_____

Business

_____
_____
_____

Spiritual

_____
_____
_____

RESOURCES

ACT. www.act.com. A great customer management system.

Ferrazzi, Keith and Tahl Raz (2014).*Never Eat Alone, Expanded and Updated: And Other Secrets to Success, One Relationship at a Time.* Crown Business

This is a great book about building relationships which are mutually beneficial for all parties interested in working together. Everyone should have this comprehensive resource in their reference library since it is such an integral part of our lives.

LinkedIn. www.linkedin.com

Meetup. www.Meetup.com
Find people here who are in your target market, develop relationships and even start your own group.

Salesforce. www.salesforce.com

CHAPTER 15

Starting a New Business

Starting your own business can be very exciting. It is also a lot of work. However, the benefits do outweigh the work if this is something you are passionate about. Make sure that, whichever direction you pursue, you keep "your why" in front of you so that when times get tough, you can remind yourself of the reason(s) all the effort is worth it.

I am no stranger to entrepreneurship. I owned my own DSHS licensed child care business in my home when my children were small, so I could stay home and be with them in their formative years. I also sold educational materials and books to child care providers so they could make great experiences for the children in their care. Now, I am writing, publishing, and speaking to improve the lives of women and their families. There is also the benefit of freedom to plan my own schedule which is quite rewarding. No matter what business you want to start, it is important to assemble a good team of trusted advisors. Also look for people who can inspire you in your chosen field. I have listed some key steps for starting a new business and then people who bring great ideas to various business models.

10 Key Steps for Starting a New Business

1. Make a business plan and get advice from a professional you can trust. SCORE is an organization that will provide you with a mentor. This organization is made up of retired executives who can help you. Please refer to the Resource section at the end of this chapter.

2. Pick the proper business structure: sole proprietor, LLC, or corporation. Consult with your mentor and accountant. You can register your business with the Secretary of State in your state. If you need legal assistance, call your attorney, or consult with Legal Zoom online for basic legal assistance. For specific business questions, look for a recommendation from someone who is already in the business field where you are starting your business to recommend an attorney.

3. Fulfill the licensing requirements from your local Department of Revenue. Physical goods require that you collect and pay sales tax. There is no sales tax on personal services such as consulting or coaching, however, there is Business and Operation tax on those funds. Check in the Department of Revenue section under resources at the end of this chapter for more information. Be sure to read the requirements for paying estimated Quarterly income tax, so you are not penalized. You can find this information on the web site for the Internal Revenue Service. An accountant is a good resource for this information.

4. Working with your mentor and looking at your business plan, determine the best way to fund your new business. When you need a large loan, check with a banker who is familiar with the Small Business Administration. For smaller loans, you may want to get started with a zero interest credit card. Be sure to check the rates that will be in effect when the zero percent time period is

over. For books and creative ventures, Kickstarter is a place to investigate. There are many ways to fund your business. You may even get creative and barter your services with other professionals.

5. Open bank accounts for your business with a banker who is familiar with small business. Some banks have people who work directly with the Small Business Administration who can help you.

6. Set up a designated business accounting system at home. I like GoDaddy Bookkeeping because it will automatically post all of your transactions to the right accounts after you set it up. Many people use QuickBooks. Keep all of your receipts and use a mileage log to keep track of your travel miles.

   You will be able to deduct expenses for starting your business, advertising, depreciation for equipment you purchase, and many other costs that you can find in the information from the Internal Revenue Service. Another expense that you may consider is Business Insurance to help protect you against liability depending on the particular business you start.

   Many people rely on accountants to give them guidance. When the IRS makes changes, an accountant can keep you informed. You will make it easier for yourself at tax time if you keep good records, and it will help with your tax preparation expense.

7. If you have a mobile or online business, set up a PayPal or Stripe account to take payments. There is also the option of using a Square account to take payments.

8. Never stop learning how to improve your business. Build relationships with people in your community and online as well

as with your customers. Networking is essential to keep your business growing. A mix of social media and in-person events can help you.

9. Always provide value and continue to be extremely helpful to your clients.

10. The most important question of every business day: What income-generating activities am I working on today? Be sure to make that the major focus of your day, and you will have success.

Yes, there are a certain amount of tasks you have to get done, but keep the balance of 80% income generating activities to 20% administrative/clerical. If you have to delegate work so you can be more efficient at getting customers and generating revenue, do it. Consider getting a virtual assistant or someone who can work on projects part-time for you.

Many businesses fail because they do not pay attention to this ratio.

RESOURCES

SCORE. www.score.org

This non-profit organization can help you with any business questions you may have and also provide a mentor if you need one for free advice and business training. The mentors here are retired executives that have years of experience.

"With over 10,000 volunteers in more than 300 chapters across the nation offering expertise in over 62 industries, we have the knowledge and tools you need to reach your business goals."

The following people have great ideas about getting started, depending on the type of business you are interested in pursuing:

Baren, Bill. www.billbaren.com

Bill is a great one to follow if you are interested in building a speaking or coaching business. He gives useful advice, holds informational seminars and webinars to give you instruction, and has courses to get you going in the right direction.

Eggen, John (2004). *Create the Business Breakthrough You Want: Secrets and Strategies of the World's Greatest Mentor.* Mission Publishing

Friedman, Marsha (2009). *Celebritize Yourself: The Three Step Method to Increase Your Visibility and Explode Your Business* www.marshafriedman.com
Marsha has her own public relations firm and has a great newsletter. How do you get into the media? Marsha has the answers in this great book.

Gentile, Tara. www.taragentile.com

Tara is a business strategist who helps you maximize your own unique business style. She is energetic and full of ideas to make your business work your way.

Loper, Nick. www.sidehustlenation.com

If you are interested in making money on the side or would like to work at home to make extra income, I recommend Nick Loper. Nick comes up with many ways to do jobs on the side that will make you extra money.

He even covers a lot of his daily expenses with his methods. Here is a link to one of his posts:

Loper, Nick. "The Side Hustle Snowball: How to 'Erase' Your Expenses with Extra Income Streams" *Side Hustle Nation*, 2016. Web. 11 July 2016. http://www.sidehustlenation.com/side-hustle-snowball/?utm_source=newsletter&utm_medium=email&utm_campaign=email.

He has written a book called *Buy Buttons* that will help you get your particular products or services in front of the people who want them.

Ogle, Sean. www.locationrebel.com

Sean Ogle is someone whom I would call a lifestyle entrepreneur. His web site is dedicated to you having a business that you can run from anywhere in the world. He has many great resources on his web site. He always gives plenty of value in his newsletters, is dedicated to helping entrepreneurs, and has built a supportive community.

Rosenberg, Ana. www.anarosenberg.com/BuildBizFast

Ana is a bestselling author and consultant to authors, teachers, speakers and people wanting to build their businesses with authenticity. She has a free course available to get you started on your own business. If you have a message that you want to get out, here is a blueprint of how to do it.

Walker, Jeff. www.productlaunchformula.com

Jeff specializes in launching online businesses and working with small business entrepreneurs. He has launch plans to help you get started and keep you going. His work will help you market any product or service you can think of. Go to his web site for free information.

FUNDING OPTIONS

Credit Cards Offers:

If you only need a small sum to start a project, you might consider one of the many zero percent offers that credit card companies give you. Then, when you are off and running, you can pay them back before the interest goes up.

Kickstarter. www.kickstarter.com

Online funding options for artists, musicians, filmmakers, and creative people.

Small Business Administration. www.sba.gov

You will find business advice along with options for business loans of various types.

Sponsorship opportunities

Companies are always looking for ideas that will bring them new customers and establish loyalty to their brands. Think about how your story and product could relate to various companies. They may sponsor your next event. You will need to research how to submit a pitch letter and develop a sponsor proposal.

MONEY MATTERS

Daily Bookkeeping:

GoDaddy Bookkeeping.
www.godaddy.com/email/online-bookkeeping
You can track all of your expenses and income here. Connect your bank accounts without giving them your account numbers and also connect sources like PayPal, EBay, Etsy, and Amazon. I am a big fan because this system will automatically record your receipts for you.

QuickBooks. www.quickbooks.intuit.com

Another option is QuickBooks if you are already familiar with their system.

You will need a way to accept payments from customers and send them invoices. These companies will help you get that done for a small fee. Shop for the best rates and features that appeal to you.

The companies are: **PayPal**. www.paypal.com, **Stripe**. www.stripe.com, or **Square**, www.squareup.com

Department of Revenue

Contact this department in your state for business license and sales tax requirements. For accounting, it is good to have an accountant you trust for advice. To keep a summary of your income and expenses, I recommend GoDaddy's bookkeeping option because it will keep track of your receipts automatically for your daily accounting and then you can tally reports to use for your tax reporting. For another option use QuickBooks.

You need a designated business account with your local bank or a bank that understands the needs of your business. I like PayPal for my business payment accounts.

A word about sales tax:

If you are a new author and are self-publishing with CreateSpace, you can get a Reseller Certificate from the state where you live so when you purchase your print books on demand from them, you will not have to pay sales tax at that time.

You will only pay sales tax once when you sell the book or order it for personal use in your state. Different states have various sales tax requirements. If you are going to do an event in another state, you can apply for a temporary permit to sell your books there from the State Department of Revenue in that state. You will then send them sales tax on the books you sold there during your event.

VIRTUAL ASSISTANTS

Contemporary Virtual Assistance. www.contemporaryva.com

When your business grows you will need help to get things done, such as web site updating, social media marketing, and copywriting. Hiring a virtual assistant for specific projects frees you up to do the things that you do best.

Upwork. www.upwork.com

A reliable firm to find help in various areas such as web design and administrative tasks.

CUSTOMER MANAGEMENT SYSTEMS

You need a system to keep track of your customers and the people you meet. There are many options out there. If you just use an Excel spreadsheet at first, that is a start. Here are some of the more effective ones. You will have to check them out and see what you think.

ACT. www.act.com/pricing/act-emarketing

I use this system to keep track of my contacts and all of the interaction I have with them. I can make notes, keep a calendar, and keep addresses and phone numbers for handy reference. I also use their group feature to segment the different events and people I meet in order to serve them more effectively. You can integrate either Gmail or Outlook for your email system. They recommend Outlook.

Salesforce. www.salesforce.com

Another robust platform for email marketing. This program is one of the latest programs with up to date technology including access to The Internet of Things which is the wave of the future.

APPOINTMENT SCHEDULING SOFTWARE

Schedule Once. www.scheduleonce.com

This software will integrate with your calendar and your website so you can get all of your systems integrated. A free trial is available.

You Can Book Me. www.youcanbookme.com

You can integrate this with your Google or iCloud calendar or both. There is a free version that you can sign up for and also paid versions with more features. You can also integrate it with your web site.

AUTORESPONDERS

You will need an autoresponder program to help you gather the email addresses of people who want to sign up to receive emails from you. You would place an opt-in form on your web site where they then would put their email in response to an offer for a valuable resource you would provide in exchange for that email.

You can then send them a welcome message or series of messages after that. You will then have them in a database for any future messages you would like to send.

Aweber. www.aweber.com

This company has been around for a long time and is a reliable source to get your messages out. I do my newsletter here, and they do have the option to call people for help instead of just an online system.

ConvertKit. www.convertkit.com

A new platform for auto responding and it only counts a customer one time regardless of how many times they appear on a list. It also allows you to send different information to different people if you have an email sequence going out. They do have free training so you can see how it works.

MailChimp. www.mailchimp.com

A free service for up to 2,000 subscribers but it will count every time you have a person on a different list as a new subscriber. Many people use this service for basic email responding.

MARKETING

There are many ways to get your brand out into the world. One of the ways to anchor yourself in the virtual world is to have your own web site. Wix.com and Weebly.com are places you can do this. One of the most widely used platforms is WordPress.com. You can set up your own WordPress site with instructions from Michael Hyatt (https://michaelhyatt.com/ez-wordpress-setup.html).

You will need a hosting company where you site will be online, and Michael will give you special pricing if you want to sign up with Bluehost. You will need to have a domain name. You can get www.yourname.com or any name that you would like for your branding as long as it is not taken.

WHEN YOU HAVE A BIG IDEA!

Launchrock.com. www.launchrock.com

If you have a great idea that you would like to test, you can make a page here and send it out on social media. You can tell people about your idea, and they can put in their name and email address if they like it. This is a free service.

Launchrock will collect those for you so that when you are ready to make the actual product, you will have an audience, or if you decide not to proceed, that is fine too. You can also use this program for a landing page for a book or product that you have already developed and send the emails to your autoresponder.

When you need a landing page or sales page for your product:

Lead Pages. www.leadpages.net

This is the number one paid service for making quality landing and sales pages. There is a tutorial available so you can see how it works.
Many people use these pages instead of a web site to promote their products and services, and they also use them in addition to their web sites to promote products and services.

When you have developed a course and need to try it out:

Teachable.com. www.teachable.com

If you want to teach a course online, this is the place for you. There is a tutorial as to how to use this platform, and they also give you access to people who can help your business grow.
There is a free platform that you can use to test your ideas and start with a small customer base and then paid features for when you start growing your customer base.

For Book Marketing resources, please see Chapter 19.

CHAPTER 16

Set Goals, Save Time, and Care for Yourself

Time is free, but it's priceless. You can't own it, but you can use it. You can't keep it, but you can spend it. Once you've lost it, you can never get it back.
- Harvey Mackay

SET YOUR GOALS

Go back to Chapter 8 where you visualized your dreams and see if anything has changed since you worked through the joy restoring process. Find a place of solitude and think about what you want to accomplish in the next one to three years. Then break down what you want to accomplish for the next year into monthly goals. Beginning right away, you can take your monthly goals and begin planning for the weeks of the current month you are in. Each week plan your daily goals using the time-saving strategies discussed below.

Here are some options:

- Print a Calendar.com at www.print-a-calendar.com has monthly calendars where you can type in your goals and print them out.

- Studenthandouts.com has hourly calendars you can download at www.studenthandouts.com/calendars/weekly-hourly-planner-printable.html.
- Mobile phones have apps you can use for planning.
- A paper version like *The Queen's Journal*, which I developed to keep you from feeling overwhelmed, uses one page per day.

TIME-SAVING STRATEGIES

When we don't manage our time, our time will manage us. Many people use the word multi-tasking and are proud to say that they can. However, research shows that as much as we would like to think that we can do it, our brains are only able to focus on one task at a time. You can read about it here in the Harvard Business Review. (https://hbr.org/2010/12/you-cant-multi-task-so-stop-tr/)

What is really happening when we are working on two tasks at once is that our brain is rapidly switching between the two and this will slow us down because it takes us time to refocus. If you have a large to-do list, find ways to eliminate tasks by delegating them to someone else, or scheduling them on your calendar for a different day of the week. There are a couple of productivity strategies that I think are valuable.

The first is to reserve your most productive time for your most important tasks. I am a morning person, so I reserve the morning hours for writing and planning tasks that require me to be the most focused. The cure for that one thing that has been nagging me that I keep putting off is to allot time for it on my schedule like I would for an appointment.

Then I look at the days and see where the appointments are and also where I can fit in other tasks like business accounting, filing, marketing projects, and meetings. Think about your meetings to see if they are truly necessary since they can be time wasters. Some people like to designate certain days for the same activities, so they don't have to worry that they won't get done.

Another productivity concept I want to discuss is something I read about called "The 90 Day Year" by Todd Herman. Entrepreneurs and business people can especially relate because of all the projects and time constrictions they have. I encourage you to try it for two weeks and see what happens. This is how it works.

We each have certain blocks of time to work each day. You have started on Task A, but then you get a phone call, and you switch to Task B on the second day. Then someone called you for a different reason, you have a meeting, and you feel you need to work on Task C on the third day. Task A is still waiting to be finished, and the distractions keep coming.

In this version of organizing your time, you would start with Task A and make it your primary focus of every block of time, with the others secondary, until you get it finished. Then the confidence that you have received from completing that task will propel you on to the next. At the end of a month, you will look back and see the projects that you have completed instead of tasks that are in different places of completion.

This worked for me when Task A was to get a book I was working on ready to send to a Spanish translator. I had other projects waiting, but I moved them to another place on my calendar and pushed on until I delivered the book. I had such a great sense of accomplishment that it helped me get the other projects done.

Each night, check over your schedule for the next day, so you will be ready to begin right away. In the morning, look at your daily planner and set your intention for the day, considering what the most important task for you to accomplish is going to be.

Block some time on your calendar for yourself to exercise, go out to do something fun, or just relax with your family, including taking the time to plan your vacation. It is more likely you will do it if you feel you have the time.

TAKE TIME FOR SELF-CARE

The morning routine:

Many people find it helpful to develop a morning routine that includes drinking water, eating a nutritious breakfast, exercise, and meditation and/or prayer. Think about what might be a good one for you. This will help you be more alert and work smarter, not harder.

Lunch:

Do you get out of your building during your lunch hour? Fresh air and a change of surroundings can give you a break from your current train of thought so you can get a new perspective. This can directly relate to how productive you are on a certain project.

I used to make it a point to leave my desk during lunch every day when I worked in the city. I would visit the local deli or take a bus down to the market to get a bite to eat. All the sights and sounds of the city would make my lunch hour like a small adventure. Maybe I would see something interesting in a shop window or meet my husband for great Chinese orange chicken at our favorite lunch spot.

The diversion away from your desk can help give you an attitude reset and keep you focused for the rest of your day.

The long commute home:

Use this time to your advantage, so when you get home, you can be truly present with your loved ones.

The evening hours:

Determine that after a certain time in the evening, you will tell yourself that you will not do anything work related and practice it often. This is one way to give yourself some space to do what is important to you and make it easier for you to rest and be refreshed.

15 MINUTES FOR YOU

We seem to be on a never-ending treadmill of life these days. Lives are very full of errands, child activities, work, and home responsibilities. The lists are endless.

How do we juggle all of this and maintain our sanity?

It seems to me that people are so overscheduled today that they don't have time to think.

Both thinking and playing are essential for our lives. It has come to the point where we need to manage our solitude or we will have none.

If you think you have no time to do anything else in your schedule, try doing something you love for just 15 minutes a day… it will make a big difference.

Here are some suggestions to get you started:

- Sit in solitude and think about your dreams.
- Write to decompress or be creative.
- Walk or run to get your body moving.
- Talk to a friend or family member you haven't seen in a long time or who you would like to keep in touch with.
- Pray or meditate.
- Dance. Yes, turn on the music in your house and dance!
- Paint or sketch a picture.
- Use your camera to capture some great pictures.
- Play a musical instrument.
- Sing.

I know you will feel refreshed when you have taken the time to relax and rejuvenate.

TAKE TIME TO BE THANKFUL

You may also want to reflect on what you are thankful for as you get ready to retire for the evening. I will leave you with these thoughts about time.

Think about the people you love, even if they seem to be causing you stress, and how your life would not be the same without them.

Take a few minutes each day to reflect and be grateful for everything you have. Keep a running list of what you are grateful for and when frustrations come, think about that list.

We recently had the horrible shooting tragedy in Florida which put many people into a state of mourning. The Tony Awards were on that night, and the actors were wearing silver ribbons in support of the victims and their families.

Actor, Frank Langella, received his award for Best Lead Actor in a Play and, instead of a long list of thanking people, he said:

"When something bad happens, we have three choices: we let it define us, we let it destroy us, or we let it strengthen us."

We can choose to move from negative emotions which will kill our ambition to positive ones that will propel us forward to greater achievement. We accomplish this by being thankful and putting our frustrations into perspective which is an excellent use of time and energy. Managing your time and emotions brings more freedom to do what is most important to you. Live each day with zest, make time for yourself, and go do great things!

Resources

Atchley, Paul. (2010) "You Can't Multitask, So Stop Trying."

Harvard Business Review Web. 21 December 2010.
https://hbr.org/2010/12/you-cant-multi-task-so-stop-tr/
Herman, Todd. Produced the 90 day year concept.

Print a Calendar. www.print-a-calendar.com

Student Handouts. www.studenthandouts.com

CHAPTER 17

Building Your Brand and Social Media

In today's economy, you are the brand that you are trying to build online. This not only applies to people who are starting their own businesses but also to those of you who work for a company. Your customers are doing business with the company because of the relationship they have with you. Not your products and services, but you. Because people do business with people that they know, like, and trust. The fastest way to see a profit is to focus on helping people solve their most pressing problems. Figure out what keeps your prospective clients up at night and give them a solution that works.

When you start your own business, you want to claim your own piece of online real estate by making a web site using your own name. In order to get started with your own web site, you will need a place to host it online.

WordPress.com is a popular option because the internet search engines pick it up readily. Michael Hyatt, a virtual business mentor, has a free screencast tutorial to help you set up with WordPress at www.michaelhyatt.com. You will need a hosting company, and purchasing through michaelhyatt.com will give you access to a discount at www.Bluehost.com. He has a blog with great business advice as well. You will want to get your own domain name.

That will be – www.yourname.com. Bluehost can help you. GoDaddy can also help you with domains and hosting. Weebly.com and Wix.com are free platforms that will also give you a place to start.

You don't need to be too elaborate in setting up your site. You will need to put your sign up or Opt-In form on the Home page, so you collect people's email addresses. You will find these forms and a place to collect them at an autoresponder company like Aweber, MailChimp, or ConvertKit. People will give you their email addresses in response to your free offer. This offer is something that is so valuable that people would be willing to pay for it, like an e-book, checklist, infographic, or other resources valuable to your audience. Email is really the most effective way to communicate with your audience, so you will want to focus on getting as many email addresses as possible.

You will need a page for your Biography Testimonials, Contact Page, and Blog, if you are writing one. You can add others as your business grows. Add links so people can reach you at other social media sites like Twitter, Facebook, Pinterest, and Instagram. LinkedIn is a great place to connect with other business people and establish a presence in your field. You can also drive all of your social media posts back to your web site by having a short bio at the end. If you are using a picture and quote, you can use Canva.com to put your web site address right on your post.

The world of social media is constantly changing. Platforms come and go. The most important thing to remember is to find the people that are in your audience and put your product or service in front of them. Find the top two for your audience and concentrate on reaching them there.

Tommy Walker has written an excellent article on how to find them in this great blog post, conversionxl.com/social-media-strategy-doesnt-rely-hope-getting-results. His process involves research and setting up a spreadsheet with all the research you find so you can best direct your efforts. For instance, on Facebook, you can search groups to find people who are in your niche. On Google, there are communities that you can search. Linked In also has groups to join, and you can set up a profile for your business there too. Twitter gives you access to people all over the world.

This will give you a more effective approach than just posting and hoping someone finds your great ideas. As of the beginning of 2017, the top three social media sites were Facebook, YouTube, and Twitter, followed by LinkedIn.

FACEBOOK

One of the most effective ways to use Facebook is to search for groups that are in your target market. Facebook might be more likely to spread your posts with relevant writing including current events.

It will be helpful for you to start a Facebook group where your members can talk with you and other people with the same interests. You can form a Closed Group where you have control over who joins it. You can invite people to join your group.

Facebook has the Facebook Live feature where you can post quick updates to your group from your smartphone. Facebook is now restricting access to your followers. When you post, your information might only reach a handful of people. Using Facebook ads can help boost your reach. Before you spend money on ads, you would be wise to check with people who have been working with Facebook for a long time. Please check out Russ Ruffino at www.clientsondemand.com for more information if you have a higher priced coaching or consulting package and want to really make this your main business focus. Kim Garst at www.kimgarst.com , a social media expert, will show you how to drive free traffic to your web site without having to pay for ads.

YOUTUBE

People love to watch videos. Relevant videos shown on your site have the possibility of increasing customer engagement. Don't be afraid to make videos. The more you practice, the better you get. Some people prefer to use a Vlog instead of a Blog. This is where you post videos about your topics instead of writing about them. You can make mini-courses with videos and give them away for free or sell them to increase customer engagement and income. Maybe you would prefer to podcast using just audio. You can find tutorials for this on YouTube.

HOW TO MAKE A VIDEO

You can make your own videos using more sophisticated equipment but for a basic video to tell your tribe about what is happening, here are a few tips.

You can use your smartphone by setting it up on a small tripod that you can find over on Amazon or eBay. You can set that up on a table to film yourself. If you need a script, you can put it on a stand above the camera to act as a teleprompter...they do have equipment for that too. Light is especially important, so aim for natural light, put the window in front of you instead of the back.

To make your video to appear that you are talking directly to your audience, be sure to look at the lens where you would be taking a picture from on your camera. You will need to do some testing to get good at this.

TWITTER

I love Twitter! You can find people in your industry. You can follow and engage thought leaders. Look for ways to be helpful to people that you would like to work with.

Provide information to your target market and let them know about your latest products and projects.

Use images that have your web site or company logo on them, so when they are shared, you also get exposure. You can make this happen by using Canva. (www.canva.com)

Also, check trending on Twitter and find out what subjects that you might weave into your posts.

LINKEDIN

LinkedIn is a site for you to post your personal business experience. This is a great place to network with other business owners by finding groups where you can build relationships. Recruiters check LinkedIn for possible job candidates.

There is also an option for you to post a page if you have a business of your own. You can connect with people by posting articles and sending them direct messages. There is more information on LinkedIn in Chapter 12.

PINTEREST/INSTAGRAM

These platforms are photo-based. On Pinterest, you make boards and post pictures to them relating to different topics. You post pictures on Instagram. Pictures are such a powerful way to communicate. To create buzz on Pinterest, you can make boards showcasing your books and/or services. Your followers will see and share your photos.

You can let people know a little about yourself. You might have a board that shows your favorite places to vacation. If you are a health coach, you could post healthy recipes or great exercise routines to attract followers. Instagram users love to follow people whose posts they admire. When you post pictures people like, they will follow you.

WHAT WILL YOU SAY TO CONNECT TO YOUR AUDIENCE?

If you take some time to consider what will interest your tribe, you will be able to engage them more regularly. What are some things that you could help them with? What do they struggle with? How could you encourage them?

Think of topics that will educate, entertain, or inspire your audience.

I write a monthly newsletter. This newsletter includes an inspirational or educational article, a healthy recipe, news, and discounts on my latest products. This way I am able to keep in touch with my audience without being intrusive. I feel that engaging people every day is annoying. There are some people whom I subscribe to that have interesting posts every week. It just depends on what you are comfortable with. The main thing is to be consistent with your publishing schedule.

I want to emphasize that being present on social media should only be a part of your overall marketing plan, along with building an email list and continuing to build relationships both in and outside the online realm.

Social Media Resources

Canva. www.Canva.com

For graphic design you can do yourself. You can make great graphics for all of your social media posts and presentations. This is a free tool to use with your own pictures. If you use one of the many pictures available, they only charge $1.00 each.

Garst, Kim. www.kimgarst.com Boom Social

Kim keeps on the cutting edge of what is happening in social media, and if you subscribe to her twitter feed, you will be able to see what is new. She specializes in getting Facebook traffic without paying for it.
Here are some of her suggestions that I like for engaging people online:
- Subtly take part in a current event to associate your brand with it.
- Vary the way you post- Use videos, photos, and links that people are more likely to share.
- Be relatable – Combine humor with experiences
- Keep in Touch – Ask a question, and be present. Comments help reach more people.
- Give them something for free – Draw on their emotion.
- Use an open-ended question to get them involved.
- Be inspirational – Use quotes.

Hernandez, M. Shannon. www.mshannonhernandez.com

M. Shannon works with people to help them develop a content marketing strategy that is in line with their particular communication style. When you visit her web site, you will be able to take a quiz to help you determine the way of getting in touch with your audience that appeals to you the most. She will help you make marketing fun!

Ruffino, Russ www.clientsondemand.com

Russ has a comprehensive plan for marketing on Facebook. I recommend you go to his web site and sign up for his latest webinar where he will explain his system, and you can find individualized help. He has helped many people who are coaches and transformational speakers become successful. In order to become successful with this method, be willing to invest in your business.

Rubinstein CHt, Laura (2015).*Social Media Myths Busted: The Small Business Guide to Online Revenue.* Transform Today
www.transformtoday.com

Laura will help you make sense of the social media maze. She gives an overview of social media strategy, helping you build connections with people in a meaningful way as part of an overall marketing plan. She is also the author of the Feminine Power Cards (which you can find at www.femininepowercards.com) that will help you keep a positive mindset toward yourself.

Salpeter, Miriam (2013). *Social Networking for Career Success.* Learning Express

The author covers how to use social media to land the career position you want. The best advice she gives is: "Don't look for a job, look for a company." Research companies that you would like to work for and see if you can connect with people within them who might be able to help you.

Walker, Tommy. "Finally, A Social Media Marketing Strategy That Puts You Right In The Middle Of Your Target Market" *Conversion XL.* http://conversionxl.com/social-media-strategy-doesnt-rely-hope-getting-results

Let's move on to creating one of the best forms of communication that will help you build your personal brand, if you are a speaker, coach, or consultant: writing a book.

ADDITIONAL RESOURCES

Bluehost.com. www.Bluehost.com

GoDaddy.com. www.godaddy.com

Hyatt, Michael. www.michaelhyatt.com

A virtual business mentor who gives great advice.
Weebly. www.weebly.com

Wix. www.wix.com

WordPress.com. www.wordpress.com

CHAPTER 18

How to Write a Book

In this chapter, we will talk about the actual process of writing your book. There are places where we will talk about traditional publishing and then have a conversation about whether you want to self-publish your book, which means you are in charge of all aspects from writing to marketing, or use a hybrid version of the two.

KNOW YOUR WHY

You first have to know the reason you are writing your book. Make sure it is a subject that you are passionate about because writing a book is hard work, and if you don't know why you are writing your book, you will have a tendency to quit. I encourage you to write down your top 10 reasons for writing your book and keep it for reference when you are feeling stuck. From there you can develop a mission statement. For non-fiction, you will want to define what you want to accomplish with the book. Susan Cain wrote the book *Quiet-The Power of Introverts in a World That Can't Stop Talking.* Her research and writing help people understand introverts and if they are one, to understand themselves better.

For fiction, do you have a series of books you want to write concerning a certain scenario, theme, or characters? J. K. Rowling uses the universal themes of good versus evil, the power of love and sacrifice, and loyalty, trust, and friendship in her *Harry Potter* book series.

In order to keep you from quitting, it is helpful to find a quality book coach to encourage and advise you. A local writers group will also have members that will encourage you to keep going.

FIND YOUR AUDIENCE

Many people write their book and then try to find an audience for it. It is best to find your audience first and then write your book. One of the best way to find out what people are buying is to check the Bestseller lists at Amazon. Find books in your niche and read the reviews there. Look for topics that those authors may not have covered and make sure that you put those in your new book. Competition is good because that lets you know that people are interested in your topic. If your niche is too small, you might not have a big enough audience.

The biggest current niches are health, wealth, and relationships. You might be writing on a subtopic of one of these. Try to find a group that would specifically want what you are writing about. First, sign up for a Google AdWords account so you can access the Google Keyword Planner. There is no charge unless you want to buy an ad.

Next, enter Keywords that would describe what people would be searching for when they are looking for your book. For instance, if you are writing a book about weight loss, you can enter that term in the planner and see how many people are searching for that topic. You will want to narrow your topic and use words that people would search for when looking for your specific book on weight loss. For example, Paleo diet or ways to lose weight fast are specific subjects. When you have found your audience, then you are ready to write your book.

Now you have a subject – how are going to know what information you want in this book? First, put down all of the information that you know about the subject.

I use a brainstorming technique called a Mind Map. You get a large piece of paper or tag board. Put a circle in the middle with your main subject or plot and characters and draw lines that radiate out from it. You can use this for both fiction and non-fiction.

Now think of all the information you know pertaining to your main subject and put each separate idea on one of those lines. These lines are your subtopics. The ideas relating to those are written on lines beneath those. You can keep subdividing as long as you have ideas.

Now, that you have your sub-topics, those will be your chapters. The lines underneath them will be the ideas contained in those chapters. Put them in a logical order, and you have a great outline for your book.

For instance, a book about dogs would have that for the subject in the middle; then the radiating lines would contain food, grooming, health, and other topics relating to dogs. Then you would put the details under each one of those headings. A fiction book would have story lines and characters along with their descriptions.

You will probably have to do research for your book. I like to keep folders with the work that I find so I can easily access it. There is a computer program called Scrivener you can find at literatureandlatte.com and www.writersstore.com that allows you to upload all of your materials so you can use them when you write. If you go there, you can preview all of the features available.

If you are writing non-fiction, you may want to do surveys to find out what people want to know about your subject. You could interview people related to your subject and put those in your book as well. You can get your spoken words transcribed by hiring someone to do that for you. A top company for transcription is www.rev.com. You can get your video and audio texts transcribed very fast and economically here. You can also search for transcriptionists at www.upwork.com. Some people like to dictate their books, and you can do that on a program called Dragon that turns your talk into text as you speak it.

Read the reviews of writers in your genre, find the topics that seemed to have been missed and include those in your book. This will help make it more marketable. My book coach, Janet Tingwald, told me that writing a book is like running a marathon. Even though it is a long journey, you have to be committed to getting to the end. If you set aside time every day to write, you will get it done. Remove all distractions for the period of time that you set aside to write. Block time on your calendar to write every day, even if it is 15 minutes.

You will need encouragement to get your book done. Here are four good ways to help you keep going.

- Hire a book coach that you trust who works with people in your genre. Ask for recommendations from other authors. I recommend John Eggen's Mission Marketing Mentors- Book Coaching if you are writing a non-fiction book and you want to get your message out into the world. Go to the link below for a mini-course on writing a book that will attract your ideal clients (www.missionmarketingmentors.com). I invested in John's program where I found an entire system of marketing that emphasizes creating multiple streams of income from my book. In addition, I participated in group coaching sessions and laser-focused one-on-one coaching sessions with a book coach.
- Join a local writers group where you can receive encouragement and feedback from fellow authors.
- Attend book conferences where you can take classes and meet book publishing companies.

USE A TITLE THAT YOUR AUDIENCE LIKES

Choosing the right title can be a challenge. However, the best title is one that resonates with your audience. Check the titles in your genre and then construct a few titles with your main idea in the title and use the subtitle to explain what the book will give the reader. The most interesting thing about this process is that the title you feel is the best for your book may not be the one your audience will choose.

To engage your audience, let them help you when you are trying to find the best one. Pick 5 to 10 titles and put out the question to your writer's group, Facebook group, or people who you feel would be interested in your particular subject. There is a great web site called PickFu at www.pickfu.com where you can get people to evaluate your title. It costs just $20.00 for 50 poll responses. They will pick between the two that you give them. You can also use title evaluator tools like the one at CoSchedule (www.coschedule.com/headline-analyzer) and Advanced Marketing Institute (www.aminstitute.com/headline). When you are done with your manuscript, it is time to find an editor.

FIND AN EDITOR

The most important thing you can do is find an editor that you click with to help you make your book the best it can be. I strongly suggest that you hire a professional editor to edit your book. There are different types of editors. Developmental editors will help you with the overall organization and presentation of your content. Copy editors will pay attention to the style, grammar, spelling, and punctuation. Proofreaders look over the final manuscript for any errors before printing.

There is a company called Editcetera (www.editcetera.com) that will match your work with an editor that deals with your subject matter. They have been in business since 1971. My experience has been great, and I would recommend them. Top editors may also be found at Reedsy.com (www.reedsy.com) where you can choose and compare various editors for the genre and get quotes. A newer organization where you can find editing help is called Upwork.com (www.upwork.com.)

Other options are to go to trusted sources like The Writer's Digest or The World Literacy Café to search. Look for editors who have worked on books that you admire. Ask other authors about who they would recommend.

Pick out two or three editors that work with the subject you are writing about. Check their web sites for contact information and see if they will look at a sample of your work so you can get a feel for how it would be to work with them. Talk with your prospective editor about your project and see if they seem to be a good fit as to the direction you want to take your work.

READ HERE FOR THE TRADITIONAL
PUBLISHING OPTION:

There are five major publishing houses in the United States located in New York City. They are Hachette Book Group, Harper Collins, Macmillan Group, Simon & Schuster, and Penguin Random House. Each of them has imprint companies associated with them for various subjects.

If your aim is to publish with one of these major houses, you now need to write a quality book proposal and find an agent to pitch it. In order to find help with both of these tasks, I recommend looking at the work of Jane Friedman who has been in the writing and publishing business for over 20 years. She has lists of resources to help you navigate the traditional publishing world. You can find her in the Resource section.

Keep in mind that you will want to start building a platform immediately, because even though your book is traditionally published, you will have to shoulder the majority of advertising.

There are many smaller independent publishing houses where you might want to submit your work. You can find a database of smaller publishers at Poet & Writer (www.pw.org/small_presses). This guide will tell you about the various houses, give you contact information and the dates of their submission periods. There is also a listing of agents that are looking for clients and how to contact them. The Poet & Writer organization has been around since 1970 helping writers and being a resource for them. You can also subscribe to *Poet & Writer Magazine.*

The Writer's Market is published every year and is an excellent place to look to find places to sell your work and gives you valuable publishing information. You will be able to find a copy at your local library. You may want to order a current version for yourself.

HYBRID PUBLISHERS

There are other publishing houses that you may run across that could offer you a contract to publish your work. They offer services that are a cross between traditional and self-publishing. They will ask you to put money upfront to publish your book. Be careful that they are reputable

and not just in business to take your money. Some of them will take any book that comes through the door, and some are more careful to examine the manuscripts they receive. You will want to investigate them thoroughly and do an analysis of how much this book is going to cost you compared with how much you project you will make. Here is a great article by *Publisher's Weekly* on the subject.
http://www.publishersweekly.com/pw/by-topic/authors/pw-select/article/70446-the-indie-author-s-guide-to-hybrid-publishing.html

A word of caution to watch out for any company that is associated with Author Solutions. The latest is the Archway Label associated with Simon & Schuster which does not mean if they work with your book that Simon & Schuster is considering your book. Please read the article below.
http://www.huffingtonpost.com/penny-c-sansevieri/-authors-warning-signs-th_b_5008425.html

FOR SELF-PUBLISHING CONTINUE ON HERE

There are several ways to get your book published. You may want your book published in print, electronic version, or an audio version. Many people love the digital versions or e-books because they are cheaper and very easy to access on their computers or electronic devices. Others prefer the print versions for their personal libraries, large-scale book distribution, or educational purposes. Those who prefer to listen to their books love the audio versions. Some people like to listen while driving or exercising.

There is a range of self-publishing companies that will help you according to the extent of help you need. It is a good idea to familiarize yourself with the publishing process. When you publish your own work, you have more control over the outcome. I have listed some of the items you want to pay particular attention to in this section.

If you want complete service packages, then you will want to find a company who will help you do that for a fair price. Many people are happy with services at Lulu and Outskirts Press. They are listed in the top ten self-publishing companies by consumers.

I have had good results with CreateSpace, which produces print books, and Kindle Direct Publishing, which produces electronic versions, which are Amazon companies. Ingram Spark is also very popular with authors.

PRINT ON DEMAND PUBLISHING

IngramSpark and CreateSpace are print-on-demand publishers, meaning that they will literally print the books when they are ordered, so you don't have to order many books that you don't need right now.

If you are want to print thousands of books for a major project, you can contact them for pricing and also comparison shop with printing companies. When using CreateSpace, you will begin to see a decrease in the price of printing on orders over 1,000 books.

IngramSpark is a very popular publisher for self-publishing because you will have access to the bookstores and library markets as well as Amazon and other platforms. They also print hardcover books. You can download a guide that will help you with publishing your book. If you have already published your book with CreateSpace, then IngramSpark will not publish to Amazon for you but will give you access to all of their other platforms.

PUBLISHING TIP: For maximum profit, I recommend making sure you get your own ISBN number and publish your e-book and paperback books with Kindle and CreateSpace first. CreateSpace will not publish your book to libraries and educational institutions when you use your own ISBN number.

You can then publish your book with IngramSpark using your own ISBN number to take in the bookstore and library market too. When you have the same ISBN number, then all of your sales will tally in one place. If you let CreateSpace give your book a number, then you will have to buy one when you move to another platform to publish.

Ingram also publishes in hardcovers, which CreateSpace does not. There are advantages to both platforms, and they do a good job of printing if you upload your materials correctly. You will have to think about what you ultimately want to accomplish with your book and where your audience is found.

SMASHWORDS (www.smashwords.com)

For all other digital platforms besides Amazon.com you can gain further reach by uploading your book to Smashwords, and they will distribute it to other digital publishing platforms like Apple iBooks, KOBO, Baker & Taylor and many more.

There is a discussion in the publishing world about whether or not to be exclusive to Amazon. In order to use some of Amazon's various programs, you must not sell your digital books on other platforms when you are enrolled.

Make a decision for your particular situation using the kind of books you are writing and if the added opportunity for an extended audience is right for you. – See "KDP Promotion" in the "How to Market Your Book" section.

CHILDREN'S BOOKS

If you are looking for a company to help you with illustrations and publish a children's book, I recommend MikeMotz.com. If you use them, please tell them I sent you. I have written and published the Sammy the Centipede series of books for children which now has four books in it all relating to children's health. You can find them on my Sammy the Centipede Books page on my web site at www.marialuchsinger.com. I learned quite a lot about publishing through this experience. They use the Kindle and CreateSpace platforms when they help you publish your book.

Mike has several illustrators to choose from, and he is also an illustrator and works as the liaison between you and the illustrator you choose to do the work.

In the beginning, you would send your text along with the description of what you want your illustrations to look like and whether they are one-

or two-page spreads and he will send you a quote back. When actual production begins, you get to approve the black and white sketches and then, later on, the color is added, and you get to approve those as well.

I was very happy with the company. When you purchase a package, they will upload it for print copy at CreateSpace and also for e-book at Kindle depending on what you want to do.

When working with MikeMotz.com or another book designer, be sure to familiarize yourself with the format of what you want your book to look like, such as justified margins, so you can direct the process of how you want the type to look on the page.

If you feel technically savvy, you could purchase the print version package. Then later you can download the files from CreateSpace and upload them to Kindle using the Kids' Book Creator Tool.

There are further resources under Children's Book Publishing in the Resources section.

Even before you have published your book, it is a good idea to begin marketing. We'll talk about that in the next chapter.

PRODUCE A GREAT COVER

Having a great cover design is very important because it is your 24/7 marketing team. The images and copy you use are crucial to success because people really do judge books by their covers.

For amazing cover designs, I recommend 99Designs.com. This is a company that allows different artists to compete for you to pick their cover design for your book. You will set up a contest and then various artists will compete. You will have a great variety to choose from. When you find an artist that you like, you can invite them to participate in the contest as well. Reedsy.com is also a place you can find top professionals and compare them before making your choice.

It is a good idea to show prospective customers your top two or three book covers and let them vote. This also works well for titles too. You can put out a survey to your favorite social networking site or group that would be in your target market. Use PickFu at www.pickfu.com to take a poll on which covers people like best.

Again, for cover designers, check with other authors about their experiences and look carefully at the work of prospective designers to see if they are a good fit for you. Once you have a manuscript you're proud of, seek out blurbs from prominent people in your field to use for advertising your book and put them on your book cover.

Your back cover copy should showcase the benefits that people will receive from purchasing your book. Check with your editor for help. There are also people who specialize in writing back cover copy.

Apply for ISBN Numbers and Library of Congress Numbers before you publish. See the Resource section. Once your book is published, be sure to register for copyright protection. You can start the process before your book is done. Go to www.copyright.gov for more information.

USE PROFESSIONAL INTERIOR FORMATTING:

When someone opens your book, you want them to be able to read it easily and have them get the same impression they would get if they bought your book from a traditional publisher.

- When you are producing any of your own books, use a publishing guide like the one from Joel Friedlander at www.the-bookdesigner.com. You can find guides for designing the interior of your books at www.bookdesignertemplates.com. Joel has templates that will help you with various formats for different types of books. He even has one called the 2-way template that makes the interior for both the digital and print platforms at the same time.
- Tom Corson-Knowles has a free course to teach you how to publish your digital books on Kindle at www.ebookpublishing school.com/kindle-publishing-training-video-1.
- If you do not feel comfortable formatting your book, you can also hire a book designer to do it for you.

- **Format the end of your book for marketing purposes.** It
will make a big difference for you. Put a note on the last page
asking people to click on a link that invites them to a landing page
for a free gift in exchange for their email address. You can host
this page through Lead Pages or connect it to your web site. Also,
direct them to your Amazon book listing and let them know you
would appreciate them leaving an honest review of your book. In
addition, direct people to links for your web site and social media
connections like Twitter, Facebook, Google+ and other sites
where you are connected.

RESOURCES

Book Coaching and Encouragement:

John Eggen

John has a program to help you write a great book and develop it into multiple streams of income. He offers a free consultation to see if you are the right fit for his program.

As a student of his programs, I can tell you that the investment is worth it for you. The program is great because you not only get individual support but the support of a coaching group as well.

Please go to the following link for more information:

www.missionmarketingmentors.com

Local writers organizations:

When you are writing your book, it is a good idea to have access to other people who share the common goal of writing a book. We all hit blocks in the writing process. Look for a writer's group in your local area where you can go for support through the writing process. In lieu of a formal program, this may be the best way to get encouragement to finish your book.

Online groups for writers:

You will find 20 different groups to join here:

Gurnett, Kelly. "20 Facebook Groups for the Writers You Don't Want to Miss." *The Write Life.* Web. 26 November 2016. www.thewritelife.com.

Book Cover Designing

99 Designs. www.99designs.com

Your book cover is the most important part of your book marketing campaign. It works for you 24 hours a day. It is crucial for you to have a great cover. It is imperative that you look for a professional cover designer. The company is used by many people with great results.

You submit your idea to the company and then professional designers all compete for your business by producing covers. You get to pick the one you like best. While the contest is going on, you can take the covers you like best and do a test with your audience to see which one they like best. When you choose the winner, they will work with you to get the cover to your specifications.

Bowker. www.myidentifiers.com

In order to properly identify yourself as the publisher of your book, you will need an ISBN number. This is a number that is unique to your book that will show that you are the publisher of your book in the directory of Books In Print and around the world. You will need a different one for each format of your book as well. You can purchase more than one at a time to keep the cost down.

If you do not have this number, you are missing out on a lot of exposure in many markets. If you publish with CreateSpace at Amazon and let them give it a number, the publisher will show as CreateSpace and not you. If you ever want to move that book to another platform, you will have to assign it your own ISBN number to show that you are the publisher.

If you are planning on printing books for profit, then it is wise to have these numbers and establish yourself as a publisher. You can use your name or the name of your business.

Children's Book Publishing

Illustration:

If you are looking for a company to help you with illustrations and to publish a children's book, I recommend MikeMotz.com.

You have the option to choose from several different illustrators so you can find the right fit for your book. They will ask you to submit your text with descriptions of what you want your illustrations to look like and then send you an estimate of the cost. They have packages that will take care of uploading both the digital and print copies of your book.

I have published four books with their help and have had good results. If you use them, please tell them I sent you.

It is best to have some knowledge about how books are constructed and also formatting when you are working with this company. Be sure to tell them that you want your type to be flush left when they print the words on the pages. This will keep them from just letting the print float unless that is what you want.

Also, negotiate into your contract to have your illustrator's name put on the cover as the illustrator instead of MikeMotz.com for a more professional look.

Additional Children's Book Resources

If you have an idea for a children's book, here are some more resources for illustrations and information:

Upwork. www.upwork.com – search for the kind of design or writing help you need.

Blueberry Illustrations. www.Blueberryillustrations.com -offers illustration and publishing packages – I have not worked directly with this company so I would be sure to ask for references from prior clients.

The Society of Book Writers and Illustrators. www.scbwi.org.

Fiverr. www.fiverr.com – Many people have found economical illustrations here. Be sure to get samples of their work before hiring any illustrators.

If you have your text and illustrations ready to go and want to upload your work yourself, you can use the Kindle Kids' Book Creator and publish it on Kindle. You will need to download the Kindle Kids' Book Creator to your computer.

You have to make sure that all of your pages are in order and in PDF format loaded into the Kindle Kids' Book Creator. This tool will put your book into the right format to upload. Then you can upload your book to www.kdp.amazon.com.
The sweet spot price for books on Kindle is $2.99.

Children's Writer's and Illustrator's Market.
Use the current yearly edition of this book to get information about where to submit your writing, conferences to attend, and publishers.

Copyright protection

In order to protect your writing, go to www.copyright.gov to register your work. You will also find answers to the most common questions about copyright protection. It is well worth the time and investment.

Corson-Knowles, Tom. www.tckpublishing.com

Tom has published many bestselling books on Kindle. He specializes in helping you get your book published and has a free course on how to do that on his web site.

CreateSpace. www.createspace.com

This is the self-publishing printing area of Amazon. They are separate, yet connected. There are many articles on that site to help you.

You can distribute to many channels here, except if you have your own ISBN number, they will not distribute to libraries and educational institutions because they require that you have one of their numbers in order to do that. – See ISBN information under Bowker in the resource section.

If you don't want to learn all of the technical details of how to upload your book, you can hire a person to do it. Check in your local area. Also on www.Fiverr.com, you will probably find someone to help you for a minimal cost. Also, check with www.upwork.com for a freelancer that may be able to help you.

Headline Analyzers:

Coschedule. www.Coschedule.com/headline-analyzer

Advanced Marketing Institute. www.amiinstitute.com/headline

IngramSpark. www.ingramspark.com

Ingram Spark has a wide variety of options for self-publishers. They are connected to libraries and major retailers. You will be able to publish digital as well as print books. You have access to hardcover copies here that you do not have at CreateSpace. They also do print-on-demand services just like CreateSpace.

They have guides that will help you through the publishing process or you can look for someone to help you. If you choose to use them, they will also give you access to Amazon. If you have already published on Amazon, that option will be excluded from your reach there.

Interior Design

The interior design of your book is also important because you want it to have the look and feel of professional design. For Kindle, I do recommend Tom Corson-Knowles if you would like to do this process yourself. He has a tutorial to tell you how to do it.

For print and also digital interior design, you can research your local area or online for a professional designer or take a look at this web site by Joel Friedlander who has been in the business for many years.

Joel Friedlander. www.the-bookdesigner.com.

Joel's web site is a great resource for getting formats for your interior book design and other publishing questions. There are many resources for self-publishers on his site. He sells book templates that will work for both print and e-book, so you only have to format your book one time, which will save you time. They are called 2-way templates.
You may also want to get a professional designer to do the interior design for your book if you do not feel confident with the options I have described.

Tom Corson-Knowles. www.tckpublishing.com

Tom specializes in Kindle books and book publishing. He has a free resource on his site that will help you format your Kindle book.

Upwork.com. www.upwork.com

This web site gives you access to many freelancers for all types of jobs that can be completed on a computer. Whether you are looking for a book designer or someone to help you with writing, editing, or marketing

Kindle direct publishing. www.kindledirectpublishing.com

This is the self-publishing digital book company connected with Amazon. You can make an account here and sell your e-books. The sweet spot price for Kindle books is $2.99.

Library of Congress Identifying Number

Also, if you intend to make your books available to libraries, then you will need to have a Library of Congress Number. You can apply for one at this site: www.loc.gov

You need to apply for the ISBN and the LOC numbers before you publish your printed book. These numbers will appear on your copyright page.

Lulu. www.lulu.com

Lulu has services that will help you create, distribute and sell your books.

Outskirts Press. www.outskirtspress.com

This company will also help you create, distribute, and sell your books. Check their web site for further information.

Pickfu. www.pickfu.com

This web site is a handy tool to get real time feedback from people who will vote on the choices you give them. You can find out which title or book cover gets the most positive votes.

Poet & Writer. www.pw.org

A valuable resource for writers to find a database of smaller presses, literary agents, and writing and publishing advice. They also have a magazine.

Pressfield, Steven (2012). *The War of Art.* Black Irish Entertainment LLC

If you ever have writer's block or a block in any creative work, this book will help you get unstuck. I promise. Steven explains the characteristics of the Resistance that we all face when we want to do something new.

Professional Editing Service

Editcetera. www.editcetera.com

This company has been matching writers with professional editors since 1971. They provide many services for writers including workshops. You can call them and tell them the kind of service you are looking for, and they will do their best to find the right match for you. You can go online and fill out a form at www.editcetera.com or call the director at 510-849-1110.

They are located in Berkeley, California.
I have been very pleased with the service they have given me.

Publisher's Weekly. www.publishersweekly.com

You can keep up with the latest happenings in the publishing world and see what new titles are coming out, and discover trends. When you traditionally publish you will want to get a review in this magazine to help you market your book. Be aware that they require submission three to four months ahead of publication and review the Submission Guidelines on the web site to work with your publisher.

Reedsy.com. www.reedsy.com

This company was founded in London in 2014 and is assembling top people in the areas of editing, designing, publicity, marketing, and ghostwriting.

There is an opportunity to read about professionals in these areas and request quotes.

Rev. www.rev.com

This program can help you transcribe and/or translate your work.

Scrivener. www.writersstore.com or www.literatureandlatte.com

This is a tool that will allow you to keep all of your materials together in one place while you are writing your book. You can then put it into a format that is ready to be uploaded onto the platform of your choice.

Smashwords. www.smashwords.com

This company will help you publish your digital or e-books across multiple platforms except for Kindle direct publishing.

Traditional Book Publishing

Jane Friedman. https://www.janefriedman.com

Jane is highly qualified to give you a book proposal critique on any manuscript that you would like to submit to a traditional publisher. She has an excellent newsletter called Electric Speed that talks specifically about online marketing tools and resources.

Jane's article on finding a literary agent:
https://janefriedman.com/find-literary-agent/

Writer's Digest Magazine.
http://subscriptions.writersdigest.com/Writers-Digest/Magazine
There are excellent articles about self-publishing, traditional publishing, how to write for various genres, and questions writers have about the writing process.

Writer's Market

Use a current edition of this book as a resource to find places to submit your writing along with publishing information. It is published yearly. Your local library may have a copy.

CHAPTER 19

Marketing Your Book

There are so many people that are selling you ways to accomplish your goals by marketing on the internet! How do you sort them out for what you want to accomplish? I am going to give you some great resources that I have found useful in my search to market my books.

One of the best books I have found on this subject is Joanna Penn's *How to Market a Book.* She is a *New York Times* and *USA Today* bestselling thriller author and she shares her experience and strategies for marketing. *The Writer's Market* and the *Children's Writer's and Illustrator's Market* are two publications that come out every year. They have a great amount of useful information about publishing along with places you can submit your writing. *The Writer's Market* also has a list of literary agents.

DEVELOP AN EMAIL LIST

One of the most effective ways to develop an audience for your book is to build an email list. This way you have people who are interested in your material when you are ready to write more or offer your courses or products. From what I have found, social media platforms should be a part of your strategy but not where you should put your whole marketing effort. Email gives you direct access to people with whom you have made a connection.

In order to do this, you will need an autoresponder to capture email addresses and reply to people who sign up to receive your information. I have a web site with a sign-up form linked to Aweber, a long time provider of autoresponding services. I also compose and send my newsletter from there.

You can make a Sales Page just for your book that is attached to your web site or make one through a company called Lead Pages which has great templates you can use.

In exchange for their email, you would offer people who sign up to your list something for free. This can be an e-book, an infographic, or information related to your book that will automatically be sent to a person upon signing up. It has to be worth something of value to them so give them something they can really use.

You can also make a web site just for your book with WordPress, Wix or Weebly if you don't have your own web site for connecting a link to your book.

Track how well you are doing with Google Analytics which can be installed on your web site. You may have to test different offers to see if you can get a better conversion rate. Your conversion rate is equal to how many people actually click and sign up when they see your offer.

BOOK LAUNCH STRATEGY

Austin Netzley at Epic Launch has put together a great launch checklist. You can visit www.epic-launch.com to get your copy and take a look at his services. Austin takes into consideration that your book is part of a strategy that can help you grow your business into multiple streams of income with online courses, webinars, and other products relating to your message. This is known as the backend of your business and can result in more income for you beyond the launch of your book. In fact, you can re-launch your book multiple times when you have a system in place that points people to your books and services.

Tim Grahl has a brilliant strategy for putting systems in place to connect with your readers, and I recommend his book *Your First 1000 Copies.*

This is a synopsis of Tim's book launch strategy for Amazon:

The best way to get your book launched successfully is to engage with people you know about eight weeks ahead of your launch date. Make a list of people that you think would like to review your book.

Send them an email letting them know about your project and that one of the most important things an author can do is to get customer reviews for their book on launch day. Tell them you would be happy to send them a digital copy of your book in exchange for their review on launch day.

About one week before launch: Send another email thanking the people who agreed to review your book and reminding them of the launch date. Let them know that all you need is a brief review of their thoughts and also to be sure to say that they received a free review copy of the book when they post their review.

On Launch Day: Send a quick reminder that today is Launch Day and a link to where they can post their review on Amazon for their customer review. Thank them for helping with your launch and to please let you know if there is anything you can do for them.

THE POWER OF AMAZON

The theory behind this method is that Amazon is not just a company that sells books. It is a selling machine that is set up to provide people with access to buy whatever they want. There is no shortage of traffic on the internet and what we need to do is get our books and services in front of the people who would be most likely to buy them. Nick Stephenson has done a great job of explaining this in his free book, *Reader Magnets* which you can download at Amazon.com. If you prefer video, go to www.yourfirst10kreaders.com and watch the series of videos. His methods will provide you with a list of readers. You can put your new system on autopilot to help ensure a steady stream of income and more time for yourself.

Be sure to go to Author Central on Amazon and set up your profile there. You can link all of the books you write to this profile so people can find out about you.

AMAZON ASSOCIATES PROGRAM

Be sure to sign up for this program so you can become an affiliate for your own book. This means you will receive money for every purchase that is made when someone clicks on your own personal link connected to your book. You will also receive credit for purchases that people make at the same time they purchase your book.

Go to https://affiliate-program.amazon.com and join. You will then be able to make a link for your book that will allow you to send people from your web site or landing page directly to your Amazon listing.

You can also make a link for products that you would like to promote in your blog that will earn you extra income as well.

If you have build a WordPress site, you can install a plug-in that will allow you to build links right from your web site. It is called the Amazon Associates Link Builder and you can go to https://amazonassociates.typepad.com/us/2017/01/introducing-amazon-link-builder.html for more information.

KDP BOOK PROMOTION

KDP Select (Kindle Direct Publishing) is a program where you agree to promote your book exclusively for 90 days at a time. During that time your book may be downloaded for free for five days that you specify to promote your book. Before that happens, plan to post on the sites where you can do it for free and get the word out to your friends and list that you will have your book available on those days. Pay attention to what category your book is in because you will rank higher in a category with less competition. You will also get a royalty paid to you when people borrow your book from the Amazon Prime Library.

A great help with promotion is Wesley Atkinson's KDROI. When you join, you will be able to submit to around 30 sites all at once when you do your free, and low-cost book promotions.

Kindle has rankings for free and paid books, and it changes every hour. You can find the rankings on Amazon where the book is located for sale after all of the book specifications on its page. The Countdown deal that includes promotional discounting while earning royalties is another

Kindle promotion. Check out Tom Corson-Knowles in the Resource section at the end of the book for further information about Kindle publishing.

SOCIAL MEDIA MARKETING

It is advantageous to maintain a presence on social media platforms where your readers tend to hang out. Do some research and look to see where your readers congregate. Due to the algorithms and changes at Facebook, you now have to pay to get a wide reach, even to the people who are part of your Facebook community.

Check out Kim Garst of Boom Social. She gives many tips and advice for free about how to get Facebook traffic without paying. She is also knowledgeable about other platforms. Jeff Bullas also has great tips on Twitter about marketing.

I do suggest that you create a Facebook community of the people who are interested in your particular subject, especially non-fiction. They can ask questions, and find like-minded people. You will be the expert to them there.

GUEST BLOGGING

This is where you go find the top people in your niche and see if they accept guest bloggers and if they do, what the requirements are for you to write a guest post for them. This is good for them if you are writing excellent content because they always need more content for their audience. It is good for you because they have a much larger reach than you do. At the end of your article, you can leave a short bio, with a link to your web site. This will generate traffic for you.

Be sure to study the bloggers you want to write for before you approach them, so you will know that the post you want to write will fit their audience. As you get to know the bloggers and their preferences, you could also suggest doing a video or podcast for them or with them.

THE LIBRARY MARKET

There is a certain process that you have to use in order to get your books into libraries.

In order to get your books found by libraries, you need to register your books at the American Library Association web site - www.ala.org.

Also, make sure they are registered with Baker & Taylor, which is the largest wholesaler of books to libraries. If you publish with Ingram Spark, then you will have access, or you can apply to Baker & Taylor separately.

If you have self-published on CreateSpace and let them give you their ISBN number, you will have access to libraries and educational institutions, if you use your own number you will not.

Librarians work on budgets, so if you approach them properly, you may get your book in the library. Let them know that you realize they work on a budget and that you would appreciate being considered for their next book ordering session.

You want to make it easy for them to order. Send them an email that details all of the information for your book including the ISBN number and Library of Congress number along with the title, price, and a brief description. Also include any awards or distinctions your book has received. Many librarians won't consider your book unless it has had a review in *Publisher's Weekly* (traditional) or *Library Journal.* BookLife is the self-published division of *Publisher's Weekly,* or *The Kirkus Review.* You will want to check out the requirements for these publications. It is important to let them know what you are doing to promote your book because librarians want to order books that are in demand.

MARKETING SUGGESTIONS

- BookBub (www.bookbub.com) is one of the best places to market your book in digital form. You offer a great deal to readers using their promotional opportunity. All submissions are not accepted, but it is worth a try because they have a huge audience broken down by genre. The best way to get accepted is to have a quality book. The company sends daily emails to their audience notifying them about limited time discounts on books that may interest them.

- Find reviewers for your books by going to the reviews of similar books in your niche and finding out who has been reviewing them. You can click on the names of those reviewers and many times you will find out how to contact them. You can then email them and ask them if they would be willing to review your book.
- If you have already published a book, revise it to contain a page at the end where people can click on a link for a free gift in return for their email address. Also give them a link to your Amazon page, and encourage them to leave an honest review.
- Write a press release and get it out on the free web sites.
- Join the discussion in groups related to your niche on LinkedIn and Facebook so people get to know you.
- Talk with bookstore managers and let them know you are a local author.
- Write sizzling book descriptions.
- Engage your audience, and they will engage you.
- If you see your book sales declining, test a new book cover first, and then relaunch.
- Check out the Amazon Associates program. If you are recommending products sold on Amazon in your writing, you can benefit from this program.
- Make a video for your web site.
- Attend a live network event and make meaningful connections.
- Develop a workshop based on your book's content.
- Make your audience smile, inform the, teach them, create something to make their lives easier.
- Get creative. Tell your brand story.
- Guest post frequently.
- Join local merchants in promotions.
- Figure out something small to delight your customers. Reward your best customers periodically.
- Look for opportunities to book yourself on radios shows.
- You may have a topic of interest to your local library, especially if you have written a book about it. Check with them and see what happens.

- With LinkedIn, join specific groups. Don't actively sell but create useful discussions and include your book title in your signature.
- For publicity, create a press kit that you have on your web site.
- Get a professional headshot and do a biography.

RESOURCES

Amazon Associates Program. https://affiliate-program.amazon.com

Baker & Taylor. www.btol.com

This company is one the largest distributors of books to libraries and other institutions besides Ingram Spark. You can register with them directly at www.pubsvc@btol.com, and they will give you information about their different packages.

BookLife. www.booklife.com

Book Life is the division of Publisher's Weekly for self-publishing authors. This is a great site to promote your work. For $149.00 you can get exposure to editors, librarians, and most importantly, other readers. There are also many resources to promote your book here.

Brewer, Robert Lee (2017). *Writer's Market*. Writer's Digest Books

Eager, Robert (2012). *Sell Your Book Like Wildfire: The Writer's Guide to Marketing and Publicity*. Blue Ash, Ohio: Writer's Digest Books
A comprehensive guide to book marketing and publicity.
www.startawildfire.com

Grahl, Tim. www.timgrahl.com

When you go to his site, you will see a place to click on Resources. He has a guide that is called The Insider's System to Book Marketing that is very helpful.

There are many titles here including helping you to set up your web site and get you started with an efficient book marketing system. He also has a book that talks about how he got his first 1,000 email subscribers.

Jud, Brian (2009). How to Make Real Money Selling Books (without worrying about returns). Square One Publishers

www.bookmarketingworks.com

This book is focused on Special Sales of books in large quantities to various organizations and associations. Brian looks into the world beyond bookstores, which can be quite lucrative. Yours might fit in here.

Kirkus Reviews. www.kirkus.com

You can get your book reviewed by the people who also review books from the top publishing houses in the country. A good review can carry a lot of weight with librarians and the public.

Netzley, Austin. www.epic-launch.com

Check out this site for a launch checklist that will help you get ready for a great book launch. Austin Netzley sets out a great case study on his web site that will also walk you through the process of a successful book launch. He also offers book launching services and has great success with his clients.

Publisher's Weekly. www.publishersweekly.com

This is where you will find all of the latest publishing industry news and reviews.

Sambuchino, Chuck (2017). *Children's Writers and Illustrator's Market.* Writer's Digest Books

Stephenson, Nick. *Reader Magnets.* Amazon Digital Services LLC.

A free book on Amazon that explains how to grow an email list.
There are also three free videos at www.yourfirst10kreaders.com.
Having an email list is a very important part of marketing. It is more valuable than any social media channel you may belong to because it gives you direct access to your customers and people who may be interested in your products or services.
Nick emphasizes that Amazon is not just a book selling company, it is a selling machine and a great way to get your products and services in front of your customers.

CHAPTER 20

Be a Great Speaker

If you have the drive and enthusiasm to be a speaker, you can make a great living! First, you need to develop a signature talk and then market to people who fit your message.

DEVELOP YOUR SIGNATURE TALK.

This talk is constructed to let people know something about you, be informative, and build credibility for when you make an offer of your services or products. Your message can be constructed in such a way that it provides value and leads people naturally to purchase from you.

You will need to build a rapport with your audience and share your personal story in such a way that the audience can relate to you and come to know, like, and trust you. This will be your signature story that you will be known by.

Then share one problem that your audience would like to solve and give them education and solutions that will help them. If you were a weight loss coach, you could talk about simples change that people could make to develop healthy habits such as exercise, healthy eating, or getting good sleep. Then let them know that you will be going into further detail in your book, service, or coaching program and you would love to have them join you.

Finally, you make an irresistible offer, so they will want to purchase from you immediately when your presentation is over.

An added bonus such as an online e-book, mini-strategy session, or bonus that would fit your main offer will encourage them to take action right away. For example, the weight loss coach might offer an e-book containing healthy recipes.

If the focus of your talk will be to enroll people into your coaching programs, then Bill Baren recommends giving a free strategy session with a compelling title that denotes value. For example: Three Ways to Your Better Health. He is a great resource person to help you do effective presentations that lead to results.

The Women Speakers Association will help you construct your signature talk and will also register you in the three major databases where meeting organizers look for speakers. There is a free associate membership and then for added service the price is a $99.00 membership fee plus $10.00 a month thereafter.

Once you have your Signature Talk ready, it is time to present it to your audience.

PRESENTATION OF YOUR TALK:

If you need to practice your talk and develop confidence, then a local Toastmasters International Chapter can help you. You may also benefit from local professionals who specialize in helping people develop public speaking skills. In my area, I found Rebecca Osman who is the founder of Your Stage Coach. She uses her background as a drama teacher to infuse her teaching, and that made her seminar of great value to me. Also, check your local community college for classes.

MARKETING YOUR TALK
THROUGH NETWORKING

Think about your target market and the audiences who would benefit the most from what you have to offer. Then find groups of people who would be happy to hear what you have to say.

YOUR PERSONAL NETWORK
See Chapter 14 for extensive information about networking.

Start with a master list of people you know and look for referrals to groups that would be interested.

LOCAL NETWORKING

Look for opportunities in local Meetup Groups where you share a common interest or ones where your book or service would be of interest to attendees. Look for opportunities that particular groups give to showcase your product or service. Become involved with the leadership of various groups and/or start one of your own.

When you have your own Meetup Group, you will be perceived as a leader in your community. This may lead you to speaking engagements at larger organizations by becoming known in your own community and getting referrals from the people you meet.

REGIONAL AND NATIONAL NETWORKING

Networking with meeting planners is a great way to find places to speak. When you start out, you may want to speak for free to get the opportunity to present your material. See if they will give you space at the back of the room to sell your books or products.

Figure out the group of people that your message would be best suited for and use Google to find meetings or conferences. When you speak to the meeting planners, find out how your message will best serve the group. When you are speaking for a fee, see if you can negotiate a good outcome for everyone on the amount of time you will speak, how much you will be paid, and whether you can sell your products in the back of the room.

You can pay a sponsorship fee to have a table at conventions and make a note to introduce yourself to the speakers that are of interest to you. You will also have a chance to network with the other vendors which is a way to gain friendships in the field with a possibility to partner with them in the future.

GLOBAL AND ONLINE NETWORKING

The WSA has a Facebook community and the possibility of doing a TV spot on their WSA-TV that will be made available to people in over 120 countries through their blog.

Sign up for speakers' bureaus online that are a good fit for you and your topic. Find organizations that need your message and contact their meeting planners.

Optimize your web site:

Make sure you include a Speaker tab that features a Speaker Sheet showing your picture, biography, and describes the services you offer. This will be a page on your web site that prospective meeting planners can download or you can send them the link. You may also want to include a video that shows you speaking so organizers can get an idea of your speaking style.

By starting local and branching out, you will gain confidence and references for future events. The best way to do that is to tailor the message to your audience. You will succeed as a speaker when you have a compelling message that people want to hear.

RESOURCES

Bill Baren. www.billbaren.com

Bill Baren will not give you a lot of hype; he will give you a lot of great instruction on how to hold conversations with people, so they will truly want the services that you are providing. He has great information on his web site and blog posts. He also has courses to help you grow your business.

I highly recommend him as a coach if you want to start your own coaching business as he will teaching you how to have productive enrollment conversations.

Osman, Rebecca. www.yourstagecoach.com

Rebecca has resources to help you with your presentation skills in her newsletter. She has workshops that can help you speak confidently in front of everyone from small groups all the way to a global audience.

Toastmasters International. www.toastmasters.org

You will find resources to help you with public speaking and where you can find a local chapter if you want to join. There is also an online magazine.

WSA -Women Speakers Association.

www.womenspeakerassociation.com
- Associate for Free or Premium for $99 a year and $10 a month.
There are many opportunities to learn from great women. You will be listed on directories of the three major speaking organizations.
They have their own WSA-TV where you can be interviewed online and then have that interview broadcasted to their network in 120 countries on their blog.

CHAPTER 21

Conquer Obstacles and Reach Success With a Coach

E very day you will do about 85% of what you always do. You have to make a conscious effort to change your mind. Many people decide that they are going to make changes in their lives and then they get discouraged and quit. They fall back into the same old patterns they had before they tried to make the change. Finding a great coach will make a big difference in your progress.

A GREAT COACH WILL:

- Help you keep accountable to the goals that you set for yourself.
- Give you encouragement.
- Take an objective look at your situation and help you chunk your goal into manageable parts.
- Listen and be a partner in synthesizing the information that you need to get toward your goal.
- Ask questions, so you can examine your own mind.
- Help bring clarity to decisions about your next steps of action.
- Look out for your best interests when others may be pressuring you to make decisions that are not in line with what you truly want for yourself.

I want to share the story of Susan Nichols. She is an Occupational Therapist who helps people with their small motor skills. Susan keeps up with the latest methods in her field and is always innovating new strategies. She was getting tired of working for other people where her skills were limited, and she was not allowed enough time to work with patients the way she wanted.

She decided she wanted her own office. Susan and I made a plan to get to her destination. She looked into the services of SCORE to find a mentor who could help her get her business up and running. They helped her with a business plan, and she began the process of getting all the necessary paperwork together.

During this time, we had conferences about what she wanted to get accomplished at certain times. I helped her think about what her next steps would be in her plan of action. This helped keep her on track. I listened to her when she felt overwhelmed and asked her questions that would help her see a clear path forward. She now has a beautiful office in the pretty town of Friday Harbor, Washington, called Hand to Shoulder Therapy. Now she is able to use her innovative strategies to help the patients in her care. Being in charge means that she can take extra time

Hand to Shoulder Therapy Office in Friday Harbor, WA

during appointments if she needs to. Susan takes pride in knowing that she is able to provide the very best care she can.

Susan Nichols (middle) with Lisa, George, and Sweet Pea
Hand to Shoulder Therapy, Friday Harbor, WA

Many people want to get their books out into the world, and Dr. Angella Banks was one of them. After listening to her tell me that she had the book written and also had it edited, I asked her why she didn't have this book published on Kindle yet.

She wasn't sure what the next steps were so we discussed them. She had her book written and edited. She needed to get her book published. She decided to get her book uploaded to Kindle first and then planned to self-publish with CreateSpace to get the printed version. I helped her get the book formatted and published on Kindle so she could get her brand

Dr. Angella Banks

up and running. Dr. Angella is a Co-Founder and CEO of Xcellence, Inc., a non-profit organization, dedicated to developing small business and encouraging youth to reach their full potential. She also coaches leaders and entrepreneurs.

A life coach can help in various situations at different times in your life. Monica Dunnagan and I met as members of the local NAPW (National Association of Professional Women) chapter. She was a student at Walden University studying for her doctorate degree in organizational psychology at the time. I helped her achieve her goal by offering her encouragement and being a sounding board for figuring out exactly what her professors required. Now I am listening and helping Dr. Dunnagan focus on her plan to navigate the process of becoming a non-profit organization that will be connected to developing an assisted living home for dementia patients.

Whatever your dreams are, a coach will help guide you to success faster by helping you overcome obstacles with support and resources detailed just for your situation.

Dr. Monica Dunnagan

Resources

Banks, Dr. Angella. www.Xcellenceinc.org

Dunnagan, Dr. Monica.
www.linkedin.com/in/dunnaganconsultants

Nichols, Susan. www.handtoshouldertherapy.com

CHAPTER 22

Encouraging Words

As I look at the human story, I see two stories—They run parallel and never meet. One is of people who live as they can or must do events that arrive, the other is people who live as they intend the events they create. -Margaret Anderson

At the beginning of this book, you were asked to identify where you were at the present moment. Then you worked on the process of restoring your joy and finding your strengths so you could find a career path that fit with your personality. Next, you found resources to help you on your new journey.

It is my heartfelt desire that you are now able to take joy in a career path that allows you to live with freedom and purpose.

Here are some final thoughts as you begin your new journey

- Figure out what you want to accomplish and why.
- In your business, remember to ask yourself what income-generating activities you will do each day.
- Keep a journal and take action every day. Write down those magic moments when it all comes together. These will inspire you when things are not going well.
- Take time to play.
- Continuous struggle may be a message that we are some place we should not be.

- Mistakes cause growth. Viewing mistakes as neutral feedback rather than failure will develop a more confident perspective of your progress.
- Reflection, contemplation, and prayer are very helpful.
- Forgive others, forgive yourself.
- Express gratitude for the past and the present.
- Quit what doesn't work.
- What causes you to smile? Write it down and think about it.
- Take care of your health.
- Action cures fear. Take action now!

Whether you have decided to take a different path in your current position or have started in a completely new direction, I would like to know so I can celebrate with you. Your story is important to me, so please feel free to write me a note and tell me about your journey. You can reach me at maria@marialuchsinger.com.

Visualize, Strategize, and Energize,
Your Dreams!

ACKNOWLEDGMENTS

I would like to thank the wonderful team who helped make this book happen. Many thanks to Melissa Stein, my editor, who gave me great direction. Thank you to Miladinka Milic for the beautiful cover design. Thanks to Luke Thomas for copyediting, Joy Burke for her formatting and production help, and Sam Arnold-Boyd for indexing.

A special thanks to John Eggen of Mission Publishing for believing in this project and to my coaches, Jill Cheeks and Janet Tingwald. Also to my coaching group who kept me on course.

Thanks to all of the following who voted on cover or title, gave suggestions for clarity, and were sounding boards for my ideas: Suzie Bauer, Debbie Desy, Betsy Diedrick, Dr. Monica Dunnagan, Nancy Sundquist Euken, Mary Ann Evango, Lari G. Leiby, Diana Linscott, Susan Nichols, Rebecca Pizzitola, Maya Sullivan, and Susan Vernicek.

I would also like to thank my husband, John, for his unwavering support, and my family for their love.

Resources

AARP. www.aarp.org

ACT. www.act.com

Act Now. www.actnow.ie

Alison's Microsoft Training. www.alison.com

Andres, Patricia A. and Eleanor A. Hill (2013). *Win the Job You Want! 7 Secrets Hiring Managers Don't Tell You, But We Will!* HigherLife Publishing and Marketing

Atchley, Paul. (2010) "You Can't Multitask, So Stop Trying." Harvard Business Review Web. 21 December 2010. https://hbr.org/2010/12/you-cant-multi-task-so-stop-tr/

Aweber. www.aweber.com

Baker & Taylor. www.btol.com

Banks, Dr. Angella. www.Xcellenceinc.org

Baren, Bill. www.billbaren.com

Blake, Jenny (2016). *Pivot: The Only Move That Matters Is Your Next One.* New York: Portfolio/Penguin www.pivotmethod.com

Block, Jay A. (2010). *101 Best Ways to Land a Job in Troubled Times.* McGraw-Hill

Bluehost.com. www.Bluehost.com

Bolles, Richard N. (2017) *What Color is Your Parachute?: A Practical Manual for Job-Hunters and Career Changers* New York: Ten Speed Press/Random House, Inc.

BookLife. www.booklife.com

Brewer, Robert Lee (2017). *Writer's Market.* Writer's Digest Books

Cameron, Julia (2016). *The Artist's Way – 25th Anniversary Edition.* Tarcher Perigree

Canfield, Jack (2015). *The Success Principles: How to Get from Where You Are to Where You Want to Be.* William Morrow Paperbacks www.jackcanfield.com

Canva. www.Canva.com

Cheapest Destinations Blog. www.cheapestdestinationsblog.com

Contemporary Virtual Assistance. www.contemporaryva.com

Convert Kit. www.convertkit.com

Desy, Debbie, The Earth Cocoon Wellness Massage, Facebook

Dunnagan, Dr. Monica. www.linkedin.com/in/dunnaganconsultants

Eager,Robert. www.roberteager.com

Eager, Robert (2012). *Sell Your Book Like Wildfire: The Writer's Guide to Marketing and Publicity.* Blue Ash, Ohio: Writer's Digest Books

Eggen, John (2004). *Create the Business Breakthrough You Want: Secrets and Strategies from the World's Greatest Mentors.* Mission Publishing

Ferrazzi, Keith and Tahl Raz (2014). *Never Eat Alone, Expanded and Updated: And Other Secrets to Success, One Relationship at a Time.* Crown Business

Ferriss, Timothy (2009*). The 4-Hour Workweek: Escape 9-5, Live Anywhere, and Join the New Rich.* New York: Crown Publishers www.tim.blog

Ferriss, Timothy (2016). *Tools of Titans: The Tactics, Routines, and Habits of Billionaires, Icons, and World-Class Performers.* Houghton Mifflin Harcourt

Friedman, Marsha (2009). *Celebritize Yourself: The Three Step Method to Increase Your Visibility and Explode Your Business* www.marshafriedman.com

Garst, Kim. www.kimgarst.com **Boom Social**

Gentile, Tara. www.taragentile.com

Glassdoor. www.glassdoor.com

GoDaddy.com. www.godaddy.com

GoDaddy Bookkeeping. www.godaddy.com/email/online-bookkeeping.

Goodnet. www.goodnet.org

Grahl, Tim. www.timgrahl.com

Guiseppi, Meg. www.executiveresumebranding.com

Hamilton, Dr. David H. "Visualisation Alters the Brain and Body" Web. 19 April 2011 http://drdavidhamilton.com/visualisation-alters-the-brain-body/

Hernandez, M. Shannon. www.mshannonhernandez.com

Housecarers.com. www.housecarers.com

Huffington Post. www.huffingtonpost.com

Hyatt, Michael. www.MichaelHyatt.com

Identity Magazine. www.identitymagazine.net

Indeed. www.indeed.com

Jud, Brian (2009). *How to Make Real Money Selling Books (without worrying about returns).* Square One Publishers www.bookmarketingworks.com

Jung Typology Test and Jung Career Indicator (known as the Myers-Briggs Test). www.humanmetrics.com.

Kay, Andrea (2013). *This is How to Get Your Next Job: An Inside Look at What Employers Really Want.* New York: AMACON

Kickstarter. www.kickstarter.com

Kirkus Reviews. www.kirkus.com

Launchrock.com. www.launchrock.com

Lead Pages. www.leadpages.net

LinkedIn. www.linkedin.com.

Literature and Latte. www.literatureandlatte.com

Livability. www.livability.com

Loper, Nick. www.sidehustlenation.com

Loper, Nick (2016) *Buy Buttons*.

Loper, Nick. "The Side Hustle Snowball: How to 'Erase' Your Expenses with Extra Income Streams" *Side Hustle Nation*, 2016. Web. 11 July 2016. http://www.sidehustlenation.com/side-hustle-snowball/?utm_source=newsletter&utm_medium=email&utm_campaign=email

Lynda. www.lynda.com

MAPP Assessment. www.assessment.com

MailChimp. www.mailchimp.com

Meetup. www.Meetup.com

Minnesota State

www.careerwise.mnscu.edu/careers/assessyourself.html.

Monster. www.monster.com

The Muse. www.themuse.com.

Make a Vision Board.com. www.makeavisionboard.com

Margolis, Michael. www.getstoried.com

National Association of Professional Women. www.napw.com

Netzley, Austin. www.epic-launch.com

New Life Coach, Inc. www.newlifecoachinc.org

Nichols, Susan. www.handtoshouldertherapy.com

Ogle, Sean. www.locationrebel.com

Orman, Suze. www.suzeorman.com

Osman, Rebecca. www.yourstagecoach.com

PayPal. www.paypal.com

Print a Calendar. www.print-a-calendar.com

Publisher's Weekly. www.publishersweekly.com

QuickBooks. www.quickbooks.intuit.com

Rath, Tom (2007). *Strengths Finder 2.0* New York: Gallup Press

Rosenberg, Ana. www.anarosenberg.com/BuildBizFast

Rubinstein CHt, Laura (2015). *Social Media Myths Busted: The Small Business Guide to Online Revenue.* Transform Today Also, www.transformtoday.com, www.femininepowercards.com

Ruffino, Russ. www.clientsondemand.com

SCORE. www.score.org

Salesforce. www.salesforce.com

Salpeter, Miriam. (2013). *Social Networking for Career Success.* Learning Express

Sambuchino, Chuck (2017). *Children's Writers and Illustrator's Market.* Writer's Digest Books

Schedule Once. www.scheduleoncc.com

Scudamore, Patricia and Hilton Catt (2012). *Successful Job Hunting In a Week.* London: Hodder Education/A Hachette UK Company

Shipman, Claire and Katty Kay (2009). *Womenomics.* New York: Harper Collins

Side Hustle Nation. www.sidehustlenation.com

Simply Hired. www.simplyhired.com

Small Business Administration. www.sba.gov

Social Security Administration. www.ssa.gov

Step, Richard – Free Online Strengths and Weakness Aptitude Test
http://richardstep.com/richardstep-strengths-weaknesses-aptitude-test

Stephenson, Nick. *Reader Magnets*
Also www.yourfirst10kreaders.com - free video series

Stripe. www.stripe.com

Student Handouts. www.studenthandouts.com

Square. www.squareup.com

Sullivan, Maya. (2015). *Dare to Be Your Own Boss: Follow Your
Passion, Create a Niche.* Synergy Books www.mayasullivan.com

Teachable.com. www.teachable.com

Toastmasters International. www.toastmasters.org

Upwork. www.upwork.com

Vitale, Joe (2010). *Attract Money Now.* Hypnotic Marketing, Inc.

Walker, Jeff. www.productlaunchformula.com

Walker, Tommy. "Finally, A Social Media Marketing Strategy That
Puts You Right In The Middle Of Your Target Market" *Conversion XL.*
http://conversionxl.com/social-media-strategy-doesnt-rely-hope-
getting-results

Weebly. www.weebly.com

Wix. www.wix.com

Women Speakers Association. www.womenspeakerassociation.com

WordPress.com. www.wordpress.com

The Write Life. www.thewritelife.com

You Can Book Me. www.youcanbookme.com

Your Stage Coach. www.yourstagecoach.com

Index

Page numbers in *italics* denote photos.

Attract Money Now (Vitale), 51, 174
audience, for books, 120, 122–123, 141–143
Author Central (Amazon), 143
authoring a book.*See* writing a book Author
Solutions, 125
autoresponders, 100–101, 112, 142 Aweber,
100, 112, 142, 167

B
Baker & Taylor, 127, 146, 148, 167 balancing
career and family, 19–23, 40, 46, 55
Banks, Angella, 159–160, 161, 167
Baren, Bill, 95, 152, 154–155, 167
Blake, Jenny, 79, 167
Block, Jay, 79–80, 167
blogging, 15, 145
Blueberry Illustrations, 134
Bluehost, 101, 111–112, 118, 168
Bolles, Richard N., 80, 168
BookBub, 146
bookkeeping systems, 93, 97–98
book launch, 142–143, 149
BookLife, 146, 148, 168
books, writing.*See* writing a book
Boom Social, 116, 145, 169
Bowker, 132, 135
branding your business.*See also* marketing
  resources for, 116–119
  with social media, 14, 112–118
  with storytelling, 26–27, 147, 151
  with websites, 101, 111–112
Brewer, Robert Lee, 148, 168
Bullas, Jeff, 145
business, starting a, 91–102. *See also* branding your business; marketing;
    networking

WSA (Women Speakers Association), 152, 154, 155, 174

Y
You Can Book Me, 100, 175
"You Can't Multitask, So Stop Trying" (Atchley), 109, 167
younger workers vs. older workers, 11
Your First 1000 Copies (Grahl), 142–143, 149
Your Stage Coach, 152, 175
YouTube, 113

ABOUT THE AUTHOR

Maria Luchsinger is a teacher, speaker, and founder of the Women's Career Transformation Network. Using 30 years of work experience in the fields of education and business, she coaches women so they can transform their careers and find joy in balanced lives. She loves to read, travel, and play the piano.

Thank you for reading
How to Get Your Joy Back!

If you would like to know more, please visit
www.marialuchsinger.com for a free e-book.

If you have enjoyed this book, I would appreciate you leaving a
review at Amazon.com.

Other opportunities available:

Destination: Transformation, an online self-guided career
transformation course. You can walk through the step-by-step
process of finding your ideal career and a life filled with joy and
financial freedom at your own pace. In addition to books, video, and
text of the lessons, this course includes a conference with me where
we will work on your new career strategy plan.

Individual Coaching Plans

Write to me at maria@marialuchsinger.com so we can set up a time
to talk about how I can support you in achieving your career
reinvention. I would love to hear from you!

You can also find me here:

Linkedin: Maria Luchsinger

Twitter: @MariaLuchsinger

Facebook: Maria Luchsinger, Coach

Group: Be the Queen

Pinterest: Maria Luchsinger

Author Central: http://amzn.to/2kbHELS

Other Books by Maria Luchsinger

The Queen's Journal – Inspiration for Action
How to Find the One for You
How to Live Within Your Means

Sammy the Centipede Books for Children

Sammy the Centipede Goes to the Dentist
Sammy the Centipede Goes to the Market
Samuelito el Ciempies va al Mercado – Spanish Version
Sammy the Centipede Gets Fit
Sammy the Centipede Goes to the Chiropractor
Samuelito el Ciempies va al Quiropractico – Spanish Version